The Union Member's Complete Guide

The Union Member's Complete Guide

EVERYTHING YOU NEED TO KNOW ABOUT WORKING UNION

2ND EDITION, UPDATED & REVISED

By Michael Mauer

Grateful acknowledgement to Pete Seeger for permission to quote from his "Talking Union."

Library of Congress Control Number: 2001095173
ISBN: 978-1-7328088-4-3
Michael Mauer is a member of the National Writers Union, UAW Local 1981.
Original design and typesetting Gerson Higgs Design, Washington, DC. Carol Higgs is a member of Columbia Typographical Union No. 101-12 of Communication Workers of America.
Illustrations by Kelly Bell.
Additional editing by Joe Fedele.
Format of revised edition by D. Bass.

DEDICATION

*In loving memory of my father, who revealed to me nearly everything about human decency
–the sanctity of picket lines, and a helluva lot more–
in what seemed like an instant.*

It must have been something to have been Joe Mauer.

Contents

INTRODUCTION

If you're reading this book, odds are you're working in a unionized workplace. Not because you participated in an organizing drive, but rather because those who came before you unionized your workplace long ago. While organizing drives take place every day of the year all over the country, the overwhelming majority of Americans who are represented by a union – probably well over 95 percent - did not personally participate in the effort. That job was done by the workers who preceded them. Since you may have "inherited" a union, you're not entirely clear about what that means. You want a better understanding of how your union works, your rights as a member, and your duties as one. You might not be convinced that you're stronger because of your union, or that as just one person you can do things that will build the union's strength or have an impact on the way the union operates.

On the other hand, maybe you're reading this book because you're employed in a non-union workplace and you're curious about what life would be like if you and your co-workers had union representation. Although this book speaks directly to unionized workers, it paints a pretty good picture of what to expect if you and your co-workers "go union."

Or maybe you're one of those people who has just gone through a successful union organizing drive. Your entire workplace is on the verge of making the change to a union environment. You'd like a roadmap of what's next and what to expect.

Or maybe you're in business school, or in management. Now it's your job to read and learn more about unions and the benefits union members have fought for, and the impact the entire labor movement has made on the economy, the world and you, even though you're not union-represented.

Regardless of where you stand, for all readers this book steps back a pace and talks about the basics of unionism. We'll examine the basic elements of what a union does, how it does it, and your role in it all, so that you'll better understand how working life is improved when you have union representation. And you'll learn what you can – and should – do to make your voice heard when your union makes decisions that will affect you.

Why learn about unions? Because regardless if you're in a unionized shop or not, unions change nearly every aspect of workplace life.

- Starting on a very practical level, everyone in a unionized workplace gets to make a decision as to whether to be a full, dues-paying member. You'll want to understand what unions do and how you fit into the picture, to make the smart decision: not just to pay dues, but to become an active and involved member.
- You can't know where you're going if you don't understand where you've been. Things are the way they are in your workplace and others because millions of workers won the fight to be represented by unions. The modern American labor movement has transformed tens of thousands of workplaces and tens of millions of lives. Unionized workers earn more money, enjoy more benefits, and have greater job security than their non-union counterparts. And, as you'll see later on, even non-union workers' jobs are improved because so many other workers have unionized.
- If you're like every other person who's ever lived, it's probably fair to say that there are some aspects of your working life that you don't like. What can be done to improve your job? Since the union is the most powerful tool workers have to gain control over what goes on in the workplace, to improve your situation you need to understand the possibilities – and also the limitations – of what a union can do.
- The labor movement has been a major force in shaping American society. When you're a union member, and when you become actively involved in all the things the union does, you become part of something bigger than your individual life, and bigger than your workplace: you become part of one of the largest social movements in America today, a movement representing over 16 million men and women.
- Finally, the fate of unionized American workers more and more is linked to

the fortune of our fellow workers throughout the world. American unions are speaking up more and more on international trade and environmental issues, human rights standards, and just about every other global issue. If employers can get away with having workers in another country do your job at a fraction of your pay and no benefits, you better believe they'll do it. And your boss likely won't care much about the true costs of low wage labor — children being forced into something resembling slave labor, or environmental concerns if a few rivers end up flowing with cancer-causing toxins in the process — if that will save a few bucks.

A Note About the Scope of This Book

People come in all shapes and sizes, and so do labor unions. There are public sector unions representing employees of governments at all levels, and private sector unions representing workers at privately owned companies. There are unionized workplaces in states, cities and towns with labor friendly laws, and there are unions in workplaces and locations where employees don't even have a legally protected right to bargain a contract. Unions have dramatically different ways of structuring themselves and making decisions.

But no matter what setting you're in, there are basic concepts that apply to labor-management relations and the role of unions. This book gives you a working knowledge of the nuts and bolts of union representation. As you read, though, keep in mind that the way things operate where you work will vary depending on what union you are represented by, what type of work you do, and a lot more. For specific answers to many questions that come up in your workplace you'll need to consult with your union, or with a knowledgeable lawyer, an appropriate government agency, or a worker advocacy group.

WHAT ARE

unions?

A union is nothing more complicated than a group of workers who have chosen to band together to promote their common interests. One person standing alone will be be weak, but many joined together are powerful.

This very basic understanding has been expressed over the years by all kinds of people in all kinds of ways. Chief Justice Charles Evans Hughes put it this way in a 1937 United States Supreme Court decision: "Long ago we stated the reason for labor organizations. We said that they were organized out of the necessities of the situation; that a single employee was helpless in dealing with an employer... that union was essential to give laborers opportunity to deal on an equality with their employer."

Not too many years later, the same sentiment was expressed very differently in song by folk singer and activist Pete Seeger:

You've got a union now and you're sitting pretty;
Put some of the boys on the bargaining committee.
The boss won't listen when one guy squawks
But he's got to listen when the union talks.
He'd better...be mighty lonely...
If everybody decided to walk out on him.

So that's the basic concept: in unity there is strength. But to understand more fully what unions are all about, let's take a look at how having a union changes some of the basic organization of a workplace, and the relationship of the people within the workplace.

Workplace Structure: Union and Non-Union

The structure and the power relationships of a workplace where there is no union are very different than in a unionized facility. In the non-union workplace, employees are simply a collection of individuals organized into groups according to the employer's needs. Workers are categorized based on what type of work they do, the location they're performing work, the shift they happen to work on, or other factors relating to the ways in which the employer chooses to get the work done. Some employers deliberately structure the work and the workplace precisely to discourage the unionization of their employees.

The employees' role in a unionized workplace is quite different. With a union, those who work for a particular employer are no longer just a bunch of individuals; they are a collective unit, as well. The union has the right – and the legal obligation – to speak with one voice on behalf of all of the employees in what is known as the **"bargaining unit."** This means that the employer loses the power advantage of dealing only with individuals, one-on-one. With union representation in place, the employer has to reckon with the collective voice of all of the union-represented workers, the union.

A Difficult Balancing Act

Of course, there's a tradeoff involved here. As an individual, you gain strength by uniting through the union with others in your workplace. By using your collective power you have greater strength to defend and promote your interests, like higher pay and better benefits. But as in any democracy, when we make decisions and act as a group we lose a little bit of individual control. For the good of the group, each individual necessarily gives up a bit of the ability to do whatever he or she pleases. For example, you may be the dude who enjoys the good company found in your bowling league, or someone who appreciates the value of being in a religious or community group. But you also understand that your membership obligates you to live by certain rules of the organization and to make some financial contributions. It's the same being a member of a union: you get the good things that come from being part of a group, but you have to give up a certain amount of individual control. As you think about that, though, don't forget this: in a non-union workplace the employer makes *all* the rules.

What can sometimes make life in a union tricky to deal with is that the group of union members never consists of people with 100 percent identical interests and needs. Within any group, there are some things that everyone has in common, like everyone in your union working for the same employer. But other things are

Working Non-Union vs. Working Union

• In a non-union setting, workers count on their own individual strength; in a union setting, workers count on their own strength plus the collective strength of the group.

• In a non-union setting, the employer makes all the rules; in a union setting, the rules are negotiated by the union and the employer.

• In a non-union setting, the employer is free to enforce the rules however it sees fit; in a union setting, workers have a procedure in place to respond to unfair enforcement of rules, even to the point of having an outside, neutral arbitrator decide who's right.

• In a non-union setting, the employer decides what employees will be paid and what benefits, if any, they will receive; in a union setting the employer is required to negotiate with the union on all pay and benefits issues the union brings to the bargaining table.

different, like night shift workers wanting extra pay for working at night, or day shift workers needing better parking. Or sometimes only one employee has a workplace problem requiring union help, such as fighting a disciplinary action. But even though it's just one person, the union must still advocate for that individual. And the union's voice must be heard, as well, for all the different smaller groups of employees in the workplace, whether those groupings are based on shift, work classification, age, how much money people earn, or any other employment-related factors.

So as you can imagine, it can get a little complicated for the union to make decisions. It's not uncommon to have situations where individuals or smaller groups within the bargaining unit have potentially conflicting interests. Example: two union-represented employees get into a fight. Each claims that the other started the fight. It can be hard for the union to sort out how to advocate for both of these union members' interests at the same time. Another example: one work unit or company takes over another, and the union has the difficult task of wrestling with the fairest way to come up with a new seniority list. Should the seniority lists be "dovetailed", or should the "new" employees be placed at the bottom of the existing seniority list? Or, come contract bargaining time, should the big push be to get special pay incentives for senior employees, rewarding them for their length of service, or should it be to raise the salary floor for newly hired folks, who usually are younger and may be just starting families?

Just as the larger society makes decisions that balance the interests of different groups – like whether it's better to use tax dollars to improve public transportation or roads, for instance – so must our unions.

More Than a Contract

When people think about the role that unions play, the first thing that comes to mind is negotiating over a contract. These collective bargaining agreements deal with what are known as the "**terms and conditions of employment.**" This is unionism at its core: employees banding together to fight for more money, better health care and other benefits, real job security, and to gain more control over their day-to-day working lives.

But unions offer much more, both directly for those they represent and as a force in society. Union members enjoy a variety of discount programs and other group benefits. If you're like a lot of union members, you purchase and insure your new car through a union discount program, you finance that car with a low rate loan through your union credit union, you fill up the gas tank with your union credit card, and you get special union travel discounts when you go on vacation. And you may even send your kid to college with a union-provided scholarship. Some unions even partner with union banks for special mortgage rates and rebates for first time homebuyers.

My Union, Everyone's Benefits

And there are a lot of other roles that unions play. These may be less visible on a daily basis, but are still extremely significant. For example, many people don't realize that the pay and benefits of workers without union representation are shaped in large part by what unions are able to win for their own members. Economists talk about a "union threat effect". This is where the wages of unorganized workers are raised because non-union employers want to head off the possibility of unionization. Even when unionization is not a specter haunting an unorganized workplace, the standards established by the unionized workers in a particular locality or industry serve to improve working conditions for all. The existence of unions boosts pay for all workers, and can prod non-union employers to provide better benefits and some sort of grievance procedure so that their workers will feel like workplace problems can be addressed. There also are laws that require the payment of wages for all workers at the "prevailing rate," which almost always means the rate established by the unionized workers in a particular trade. The best-known of these is the Davis-Bacon law, which applies to federally funded construction projects.

On an even broader scale, the actions of unions in the legislative arena end up protecting all employees, and indeed all people in our country. Many laws that benefit everyone would not have been passed without the efforts of organized labor. The establishment of our Social Security system is probably the most important of these. But there are hundreds of other examples of legislation that transformed American society in which organized labor was a key factor, including workplace health and safety and anti-discrimination laws, Medicare, and unemployment compensation.

> ### It's All Connected
>
> "Our needs are identical with labor's needs–decent wages, fair working conditions, livable housing, old age security, health and welfare measures, conditions in which families can grow, have education for their children and respect in the community. That is why Negroes support labor's demands and fight laws which curb labor. That is why the labor-hater and labor-baiter is virtually always a twin-headed creature spewing anti-Negro epithets from one mouth and anti-labor propaganda from the other mouth."
>
> –Dr. Martin Luther King, Jr., speaking in support of striking sanitation workers in Memphis, April 3, 1968

Union Movement = Social Justice Movement

Some of organized labor's proudest moments have come at those times in American history where unions took the lead in a fight to improve our society. Martin Luther King, Jr., the Nobel Prize-winning advocate for civil rights, was gunned down in Memphis in 1968, a day after delivering his "I've Been to the Mountaintop" speech. But how many Americans know that what brought Dr. King to Memphis was the melding of a labor union contract fight and the growing force of the civil rights movement? In a key moment in both union and civil rights history, African-American sanitation workers organized by the American Federation of State, County and Municipal Employees (AFSCME) were on strike for union recognition and for dignity, united by the slogan "I Am a Man." While strikers were on the picket lines, community supporters pitched in with a boycott of downtown merchants led by the local NAACP and African-American ministers. Dr. King traveled to Memphis because he understood that the union fight to improve wages and benefits and to get dignity on the job was a part of the larger struggle to create a society where Americans of all races and nationalities would be treated equally, saying:

"You are demanding that this city will respect the dignity of labor. So often we overlook the work and the significance of those who are not in professional jobs, of those who are not in the so-called big jobs. But let me say to you tonight that whenever you are engaged in work that serves humanity and is for the building of humanity, it has dignity and it has worth."

And there long has been recognition on the union side, as well, that our fight for improved working conditions is connected to the social justice movement in the larger society. One of the few non-African-Americans invited to speak at the historic 1963 March on Washington for Jobs and Freedom was Walter Reuther, president of the United Auto Workers union (UAW).

> *"We in the UAW have been in the forefront of every basic struggle in the country, and we have learned some very simple, fundamental truths; that you cannot solve a human problem by pitting one human being against another human being. We have learned that the only way you can solve human problems is to get people to join hands and to find answers to those problems together. And it's for this reason that we reject the voices of extremism in America, whether they be white or black; for there are no separate answers. There are no white answers to the problems, there are no black answers; there are only common answers that we must find together in the solidarity of our common humanity.*
> *– Walter Reuther, addressing the 1970 UAW Convention*

Not a Spectator Sport

Unions are more than a kind of employment insurance policy for working people. True, one face of unions is that they are an organization to which dues are paid regularly. Just like insurance premiums that are paid to insurance companies, these dues buy help in the event that something goes terribly wrong on the job.

But unions are capable of accomplishing a lot more than that. Plenty of union members and union officials have learned the hard way what happens when workers come to think of their union only as a business that provides a service. Rather, it's a group of people banding together to fight for common interests, and that's what gives the union the clout and credibility needed to defend and advance the members' interests. When an employer looks and sees only a small handful of paid union staff or elected union leaders and no one standing behind them, pretty soon the employer starts thinking that "the union" isn't really much to contend with. And the truth is, that's right.

Chapter
Two

HOW YOUR

union operates

You may be in an independent union that represents just a small number of folks in a single workplace. If that's the setup you have, then what you see is what you get: your union is the sum total of you and your co-workers, choosing leaders in your workplace among yourselves, and taking unified action. You have no connections with a national union, like the American Federation of Teachers (AFT) or the Teamsters or any of the scores of others. And you are not affiliated with a national labor federation, either the American Federation of Labor-Congress of Industrial Organizations (AFL-CIO) or Change to Win (CTW.)

Chances are, though, that you are in a union local that is part of a much larger organization with many different levels. Unions come in all shapes and sizes, and just as the political structure of one American city might vary greatly from that of another, different unions govern themselves in different ways.

But there are some basic ways that unions are structured. So let's take a look at how your union is likely to be set up in your particular work unit, and work our way up to – truly – the international level.

The Workplace View

The heart and soul of any union is its members, and they are pulled together by a network of first-line union representatives, often called "**stewards.**" Your union may use a different title for this position, such as department rep or representative spokesperson, but the functions will be the same. Stewards are the "eyes and ears" of the union, keeping track for the union of what's happening on a day-to-day basis. An effective steward functions as a two-way pipeline: passing information along to higher-ups in the union so that they can formulate plans to respond to employer actions, and making sure that the union members in their areas are kept informed about what's going on within the union.

There is no set rule for how many stewards you'll find in a particular workplace, or how many will have responsibility for particular work areas. Sometimes there is a natural organization of the workplace – such as a well-defined work unit, or a particular work shift or one building separated from the rest of a larger facility – so that it makes sense for stewards to be assigned on that basis. It may be that stewards where you work function according to workplace geography. A steward may be responsible for all union members on a particular floor of a building, for example. Or your steward may handle matters that directly affect everyone who does your type of job, such as all accountants in a particular government agency, or all nurse's aides on a particular wing of a nursing home. Or maybe your steward deals with everyone who works on your shift.

Stewards come to be stewards in many different ways. Some unions conduct elections to choose stewards to serve for a specific term of office. In other unions, stewards are appointed, either for a set period of time or indefinitely. Stewards sometimes can spend time during working hours to do their union business while still getting their regular pay. Some unions provide a stipend for stewards to compensate them for the extra hours and effort they put in representing members. Stewards will often be assembled for regularly-scheduled meetings to get briefed on developments that affect individual members or the labor movement as a whole, and to talk through what issues the union needs to address.

Regardless of the formal method for selecting stewards in your workplace, it may well be that most are serving simply because they volunteered. With most unions offering at least some fundamental training in how to do the job of steward, you might want to think about stepping up and playing a more active role in your union in that way.

Union Stewards: First to be Asked

Your steward is your first point of contact when you have a question about whether your workplace rights have been violated, or when you have an idea about some union action that might improve conditions in your workplace. You can't expect

Employee Involvement Programs

Most of what unions do, and what most of what this book explains, addresses the essential "us and them" power relationship in the workplace. Without a union, individual employees are at a big disadvantage in trying to protect their interests against a powerful employer. Unions speak collectively for all those in a bargaining unit, negotiating contracts and challenging employer actions through grievances and other means.

But in an increasing number of workplaces, a different structure for labor-management relations has taken hold. These are sometimes in place of the traditional adversary mechanisms and sometimes alongside them.

These employee involvement programs are devices by which employee and employer representatives sit side by side (both literally and figuratively) to tackle workplace concerns. In some instances, they have proven to be a valuable means for employees collectively to have significant input into workplace decisions. For example, there may be topics that an existing union has no legally-enforceable right to negotiate, but the union gets a seat at the table through these programs.

But be aware that serious dangers can arise. Some employers establish and manipulate these groups as part of a deliberate strategy of divide and conquer. The idea is that by setting up a forum where the voices of individual employees are heard, the union's role as the collective voice for all its members is weakened. And some union leaders and members discover the hard way that after a period of "cooperation" with the employer, they are unable to challenge a damaging employer initiative because they failed to preserve the union's contract and other rights. Unless clear limits are set on the authority of employee involvement programs, the union and its members can find themselves back in the position of being powerless to affect the important decisions in the workplace.

a co-worker who has become a union steward to be an expert on all aspects of workplace rights. But it is a steward's responsibility to do what it takes to find out, if necessary, what action may be appropriate to challenge an employer initiative and to safeguard employees' rights.

Many questions or problems you bring to your steward can be dealt with satisfactorily without any type of formal action being taken. It may be that information is the fix that's needed, or a conversation between your steward and a management official solves the problem. But sometimes a steward will set in motion a formal action, the most common type being a contract grievance. Your problem or concern calls for a grievance to be filed, then your steward may serve as a "mini-lawyer" who will help draw up and present the grievance and attempt to get it resolved What is grievable and what's not, and the procedures used, are covered in some detail in Chapter 7.

Your steward may take another type of action as well to assist you. Your steward is the one with overall responsibility for answering questions about what the employer or the union is doing or could be doing to make things better in the workplace. If the union cannot do something to bring about positive change, your steward should be able to explain why that is.

One Level Up in Your Union

Above the level of steward, the structure of unions varies greatly. But however it is designed, the union in your workplace will be set up in such a way that information is collected, decisions are made, and actions are taken.

It may be, for example, that all of the individual stewards in your workplace report to a chief steward. This person has the responsibility for coordinating all of the grievance activity, including recommending which cases get processed all the way to arbitration – a step taken if the union and the employer can't work out a way to settle an important grievance.

Or your union may have a workplace committee structure, where a "**grievance committee**" or a "**representation committee**" coordinates all such work. Other union committees may have the responsibility for gathering and passing out information and taking necessary action on a range of other matters, such as health and safety, legislative affairs, or human and civil rights. And sometimes matters such as health and safety are dealt with by joint labor-management

Shared Governance = Co-Determination?

In some western European countries, particularly Germany, there's a model of "works councils" and "co-determination." These allow employee representatives to have a direct voice in workplace decision-making and even have designated seats on the employer's governing board. These structures exist across the economy, including in traditional industrial workplaces.

In the United States, setups providing for such direct participation by employees historically have been limited to just one or two corners of the economy. The most widespread of these is on college and university campuses, where there's almost always a structure of shared governance. Faculty (and sometimes other campus workers) participate in a formal body with defined powers that meets regularly, and that can speak up and participate jointly with the administration on a range of matters of concern. In this way, the academic workers get a seat at the table to deal with much more than just wages, benefits, and working conditions. They get to be a key player in shaping how their workplace is run, including having heavy influence on academic decision-making, such as what courses and majors will be offered.

Some American unions are now exploring starting down the road to unionization by getting other types of employers to agree to a co-determination setup. And as U.S. unions solidify their ties with unions in other countries where a particular employer does business, the European-based unions have helped pressure the employer to agree to the same type of labor relations policy in this country that the employer practices in Europe. One good example is what's happened in the auto industry. The largest German labor union in the auto industry, IG Metall, has been a loyal partner to its American counterpart. The German union has pressured auto manufacturers who set up shop in the U.S. to back off from the kind of open hostility towards union organizing that is much more common in the U.S. than in Europe. And IG Metall has lent a hand to the United Auto Workers as it explores establishing the kind of co-determination programs in U.S. manufacturing facilities that are common in European plants.

committees, consisting of representatives of both the employer and the union.

Every local has officers, most likely serving for particular terms that are specified in your union constitution and bylaws, and most likely governed by legal requirements as to election procedures and other aspects of the union's business.

Unions label themselves in different ways. Most commonly you'll see "**Local**" followed by a number designation. Other times you'll see "chapter," or "lodge" or "branch." Sometimes it's more than one workplace that's represented by a single local union. For example, it may be that the social workers at a number of different hospitals have unionized, and have negotiated contracts for each hospital. But they may all be in a single citywide or statewide union local. In any event, based on geography or your type of industry or work, your union local is connected in some way with other locals. It may be, for example, that all of the locals of a union in a particular city, county, or even state or larger geographical area, unite organizationally to deal with common issues. They can be more effective in addressing concerns they share, or even negotiating jointly, on this broader basis. Or your union may be set up so that different locals representing the same type of employees – such as all county employees, or all of a municipality's blue-collar employees – will be combined organizationally. So your local might be part of a larger structure called a District Council, a Council of Chapters, or something similar.

And at one level or another in your own local union if it is large enough; or if it's small, then on a regional or national union level – your union will have staff employees doing the full range of union work. Union staff may handle grievance/arbitration advocacy, bargaining, membership growth, enforcing health and safety standards, or even in-house lawyering. Some union staff are drawn from among the people represented by the union, while others are individuals who have chosen union staff work as their livelihood.

National Connections

You most likely are part of a national union, too. If your union is called an "**International**," this means that there are members outside of the fifty states, most often Canada or Puerto Rico. The national officers of your union serve for lengths of time determined by the union constitution and bylaws, and sometimes by law. Some unions conduct elections for national officers the same way most other elections are conducted: by secret ballot, usually with each member eligible to cast a vote by mail or electronically. Other unions choose to elect their officers at a convention, with delegates usually casting votes based on the number of people they represent. Your national union will also have a fairly sizable governing body, called a Council, Executive Board, or something similar. As with the larger components of the union at other levels, the national union will have paid, full-time staff working with the officers to implement the union's program. At the national level as well there is likely to be a committee or departmental structure of some sort, where the work of the union in a particular area (such as legislative work or new organizing) is coordinated.

As a way to combine their resources, increase effectiveness and, in part, to respond to mergers and takeovers on the part of employers, sometimes unions agree to their own mergers and affiliations with other unions. In some instances, unions representing workers who perform very similar types of work have decided that it makes more sense to have one bigger union than two smaller unions. One example of this was the merger of the Screen Actors Guild and the American Federation of Television and Radio Artists to form SAG-AFTRA. In other instances, union mergers are responses to changes in an industry itself. For example, with new technologies there is increasingly a single information industry, replacing the separate, more distinct enterprises of newspaper journalism, the printing trades, and other types of mass communication. To respond to this, a number of smaller unions, including the NewsGuild, the Electronic Workers, the Broadcast Employees and Technicians, and the International Typographical Union are now all part of the Communications Workers of America (CWA.)

Unions Work Together

The **American Federation of Labor-Congress of Industrial Organizations (AFL-CIO)** is an umbrella organization of more than 50 American unions. The smaller **Change to Win (CTW)** federation consists of four additional national unions. Some other unions, such as the National Education Association (NEA), the National Treasury Employees Union (NTEU) and the United Electrical Workers (UE), have chosen to remain independent. Together, unions in the U.S. represent over 16 million workers. Just as businesses band together in chambers of commerce, through the AFL-CIO most American unions at the national level are able to work together on a wide range of common concerns. With officers elected at a convention of AFL-CIO affiliated unions, and a sizable staff based in Washington, D.C., the AFL-CIO speaks with one voice for the interests of American workers of all types and their unions. Research is done at the national level on areas of concern to working people, analysis of government and social policy is undertaken, ambitious political involvement is coordinated, and efforts are made to mesh the bargaining and organizing agendas of the various affiliated unions. Separate departments seek to zero in on areas of concern to particular types of workers, such as professional employees or those in the building trades. And some projects are undertaken at the national level, such as coordinating the bargaining of all affiliated unions representing workers at a particular company.

Below the national level, too, your union probably has connections with other unions or with other organizations with compatible goals. Often more than one union will represent different types of employees at a single employer (or even in a single facility). In such cases, the different locals often realize that they will have more power if they work cooperatively. This can take a number of different forms. For example, there may be regular meetings of the different locals, simply to share information about what the employer is up to and what locals are doing to protect their members' interests. Some locals band together to take effective joint action, such as coordinating their bargaining, so that the employer cannot easily play off one group against the others.

On a geographical basis, unions often have ongoing organizational relationships. For example, the AFL-CIO has **State Federations** and **Central Labor Councils**, which are networks of the different unions that represent employees in a particular city, county or state. These combine their member unions' work on political matters (such as endorsing or campaigning for a particular candidate, or fighting for or against proposed legislation), and support one another in organizing drives or in battles with a local employer.

Alt Labor: A New Twist on Organizing

A number of American unions including both national federations, the AFL-CIO and Change to Win, have supported and partnered with a variety of workers' centers that are practicing a new type of organizing designed to create better pay and working conditions. *(continued on next page)*

These "**alt-labor groups**" (sometimes called non-traditional unions) are community-based organizations that provide services and do advocacy work on behalf of certain categories of workers. Often, the focus is on groups of workers who may lack the legally protected right to unionize: domestic workers, farm laborers, and others labeled "independent contractors." There's also the full range of workers in the new gig economy, those who find work as drivers or making deliveries of groceries or packages. Whether it's the unavailability of good, stable jobs or the need to have a second income or a flexible work schedule, increasing numbers of workers are doing such on-demand work. The constituencies of what are often called "**worker centers**" often are the most exploited segment of workers in America, primarily immigrants. Sometimes the focus of these groups is on legislative fixes to problems that working people face: things like fighting for legal protection against wage theft, or for a living wage, rather than the low minimum wage that keeps people in poverty. Sometimes the focus is on particular employers, turning up the heat so that conditions are improved for their workers.

Often the fight is multi-employer, and there are some notable success stories that have come out of this. One involves farmworkers in Florida, where 90% of our winter tomatoes are grown. The Coalition of Immokalee Workers ran a campaign to get food industry giants to pledge to buy only from growers who meet standards that provide for better quality jobs for the tomato pickers. One by one, huge companies agreed: McDonalds; Yum (which owns Taco Bell, Pizza Hut and KFC); and finally the world's largest retailer, Walmart. Thanks to that campaign, the 30,000 workers who produce 90 percent of Florida's tomatoes enjoy higher wages and work in fields that adhere to strict standards that mandate rest breaks and forbid sexual harassment and verbal abuse.

Unions' support of these kinds of advocacy groups is part of the larger strategy for advancing the interests of working people. Just as unions choose to join their efforts with those of other unions in order to increase their strength and effectiveness, unions forge partnerships with community organizations to further our common cause. Quite often, it's the advocacy groups themselves who first reach out to form alliances with organized labor, and give unions the prod they need to broaden their efforts to address inequities in the workplace and in the community.

Unions Form Alliances

Labor unions share countless goals with other organizations: strong public education, affordable health care for all, environmental responsibility, voting rights, a fair immigration system, and many more. We saw how labor unions and the civil rights movement joined forces in the 1960's under Dr. King's leadership to build a strong union for the sanitation workers in Memphis. In contemporary America, unions forge alliances with a wide variety of community, civic, religious, environmental and political action organizations with whom we have common interests.

So perhaps your union local has joined forces with student groups to bring a halt to products made with sweatshop labor being sold on campuses. Or you've gotten involved in a living wage campaign to set a truly decent hourly pay rate for all workers in your city. Or your union works side by side with environmental activists to fight for new jobs in wind, solar, and other clean energy sources, or with immigrant advocates to beat back the kind of exploitation of workers that undercuts all working people's job security. Whatever the details, the principle is the same one that leads to the formation of unions in the first place: in unity, there is strength.

International Connections

Increasingly, companies operate in many different countries, and each country's national trade policy is determined by what goes on everywhere in the world. Nearly every day we can read in the newspaper about a US company pulling up stakes and moving call centers or other parts of its operation to another country (or blackmailing workers and communities by threatening to do so.) Sometimes the last days on the job for an American worker involve training a foreign counterpart in how to do the work, because the employer has decided to take advantage of the ability to get someone else to do the work at lower cost.

Unfortunately, American workers have lots of direct experience with how jobs move abroad as companies seek cheaper, non-union labor. Large parts of some American industries, and lots of jobs in certain parts of the U.S. have relocated to less developed nations as business owners seek higher profits. American unions have fought this in a variety of ways, including lending a hand to their Third World brothers and sisters who fight for workplace rights. It's a pretty basic equation: if workers in other countries can win workplace standards more in line with our own, American employers will have less incentive to move our work overseas.

It's worth keeping in mind that sometimes this same phenomenon takes place in the other direction, too. Auto manufacturers in particular have seized upon the competitive economic advantages in opening plants in the U.S. rather than in Western Europe. A manufacturing plant in the U.S. south or another less union-friendly part of the country can give a company in search of maximum profits a non-union workforce. Substituting nonunion American workers for unionized Europeans can allow the company to set a lower wage scale and level of benefits, and there will be fewer legally required employment rights (like paid time off for having kids.) As a result, labor unions in other parts of the world have lent support to workers in this country seeking improvements in workplace standards or specifically to unionize. It's not just a case of them "doing the right thing." Those unions in Europe and elsewhere understand that they can protect the quality of their own jobs if they prevent employers from undercutting European living standards by using non-union American workers.

Fierce political fights have broken out over what kind of restrictions should be placed on international trade and the mobility of international capital and labor. We've seen hard-fought disputes over adoption of trade pacts like the North American Free Trade Agreement (NAFTA) and the Trans-Pacific Partnership (TPP), and over trading relations directly between the U.S. and some individual countries. At the heart of these from the business point of view is their ability to use workers in other countries who can be paid much less than their American counterparts and won't be able to unionize. Labor's goals for these trade pacts is to level the international playing field, so that big business can't play off one

---

Globalization and Inequality

Former Treasury Secretary Lawrence Summers has identified one negative effect of increasing globalization on U.S. workers: "The consensus view now is that trade and globalization have meaningfully increased inequality in the U.S. by allowing more earning opportunities for those at the top and exposing ordinary workers to more competition, especially in manufacturing."

group of workers against another in a race to the bottom that ends up hurting all working people, regardless of nationality. Labor fights to have these trade pacts include protections for workers in the affected countries to be able to join free and independent trade unions. These fights also illustrate the cooperation between organized labor and our allies, as we join forces with groups demanding that environmental protections be incorporated into these trade pacts.

And so it's a necessity for unions to combine their efforts across national borders. In order to respond effectively to these challenges, American unions participate in the world's largest union organization, the **International Trade Union Confederation (ITUC)** – "the global voice of the world's working people" – and its regional organizations. Under this umbrella, over 200 million workers in more than 160 countries have joined forces. And in **Global Union Federations (GUF)**, unionists from every continent who work in the same industry coordinate their efforts. For example, the American labor unions representing those in the food and beverage industry are part of a group called the International Union of Food, Agricultural, Hotel, Restaurant, Catering, Tobacco and Allied Workers' Associations (IUF), to which over 400 labor unions from 130 countries belong. Organizations participating in these Global Union Federations also include some independent American unions, who are not affiliated with the

Samuel Gompers

Born into a Jewish family in London, Gompers began his working life at the age of 10, rolling cigars. When he was 13 his family immigrated to the United States, where Gompers began his union life in the United Cigar Workers union. His career in the labor movement oversaw a huge increase in the size and influence of American labor unions, with the AFL growing from 50,000 members in 1886 to nearly 3 million in 1924. On May Day in 1886, he led the way in a nationwide general strike in support of establishing an eight-hour workday. You may want to sit down before reading this statistic: in 1890, when the government first tracked workers' hours, the average workweek was 100 hours for full-time manufacturing employees and 102 hours for building tradesmen. Gompers was an instrumental figure in establishing the 40 hour workweek and molding the working rights we all have today.

AFL-CIO. Education International, for example, includes the National Education Association and its nearly 3 million members. To advance their efforts on behalf of the millions of workers they represent, unions from all over the world exchange information through the Global Union Federations and come up with common positions and actions that will benefit their members worldwide. And they enter into formal Framework Agreements with multinational corporations to get those companies to adhere to universal standards of job protection and to respect the right of workers to organize.

International Labor Solidarity: A Two-Way Street

As employers have operated on a more and more global basis, unions in different countries meet that challenge by doing the same thing. The story of Zara, the world's largest clothing manufacturer, illustrates this well.

Zara, a Spanish company, set up shop in a number of locations in Manhattan. This was part of a trend in the apparel industry where European manufacturers move their operations to the U.S., expanding their use of part-time workers with less job security and lower wages and benefits. The U.S. Zara workers, understandably, wanted to improve the quality of their jobs and their worklife, so they began to work with the Retail Workers Union (Retail Wholesale and Department Store Union, RWDSU) and with a New York City worker center. Their #ChangeZara campaign focused public attention on how differently Zara treated its unorganized U.S. workforce and its unionized European workers. After much escalating agitation, including confronting management with petitions and holding public rallies, Zara agreed to increase the number of full-time positions, end on-call shifts, and give workers a raise.

But this wasn't enough for the Zara workers. So the campaign kept turning up the heat, fueled by international pressure being applied to Zara. Key to that pressure was that Zara's parent company had signed on to a Framework Agreement. In the end, the company agreed to a hands off policy on the U.S. organizing effort and pledged that it would recognize a union if a majority of its New York workers demonstrated that they wanted one. With company opposition out of the picture, a majority of the workers quickly signed union cards. The new union achieved formal recognition and began negotiating its first collective bargaining agreement.

A
member's rights
AND RESPONSIBILITIES

Since you're working in a unionized workplace, because of its role as "**exclusive representative**," your union is entitled – in fact, is required by law – to represent every individual in the bargaining unit. But the flip side of that coin is missing; the law says that you can choose not to be a full, dues-paying member. Depending on a variety of factors, including what your union contract provides, it may be that the most you can be required to pay is a portion of the full dues amount. If you are a public sector employee, thanks to the ruling by the U.S. Supreme Court in the *Janus* case (more about this below), you can even get away with paying nothing at all. If that sounds tempting, you might want to think about other ways you could save a few bucks: not spending money to replace bald tires (a good idea until you hit a slippery stretch of road), or holding off on fixing your leaky roof (no problem, until a heavy rain comes along), or not getting your flu shot (just fine, until you come down with the flu.)

Practical Aspects of Membership

Before going into an explanation of the different categories of what are called "**union security**" arrangements, let's take a look at why becoming a full, dues-paying union member is the right thing to do.

You Get to Participate in Decision Making

Paying union dues is your ticket to having a say in what the union does. Just as when we get fed up with the voting record of one of our elected legislators and we "vote the bums out" in the next election, union members have the same system of checks and balances for union officers. If you're dissatisfied with the quality of union leadership, the solution is to support other candidates in the next elections. But you get to vote *only* if you're a dues-paying member.

And around contract bargaining time, only dues-paying union members are eligible to participate in making many critical decisions. For example, many unions conduct a pre-bargaining poll – but only of members – to determine priorities at the bargaining table. Sometimes unions will hold Contract Proposal Meetings where members get to weigh in on what they'd like the new contract to contain. And virtually all unions permit only full, dues-paying members to vote on whether or not to ratify the final contract agreement that the negotiators have reached. No membership, no say in the process. No membership, no right to vote on the outcome.

You send a message

Union officials and staff members keep a very close watch on the number of represented employees who choose to join the union and pay full dues. Savvy union leaders also understand that there's someone else who is keenly interested in how many choose to join and how many try to freeload: the boss. Those on the other side understand full well that the more limited the union's resources, the less effective it will be. A strong, voluntary union membership gets the message across to the employer that the individual employees are standing behind their leaders. That way, when a union official addresses the employer, it's understood that one voice speaks for many.

Everything Costs Something

The ultimate strength of the union lies in the determination and participation of its members. But it's also true that it takes money for an organization to translate good intentions into concrete actions. What use is negotiating a collective bargaining agreement with strong protections if the union doesn't afterwards have the money needed to process grievances to arbitration when the employer chooses to ignore what the contract says? How effective can your union be if there is no money to pay rent for office or meeting space, to hire knowledgeable staff to answer your questions on the phone, or to bring in health and safety experts to advise on hazards in the workplace? Everyone needs to pitch in financially to make the union strong.

Information Is Power

Your union probably provides more comprehensive information to dues-paying members than to other represented employees. Some of this is based on fairness: those who are footing the bill for the organization's work deserve more detailed information on what the organization is doing. But some of this is also an outgrowth of the union having to choose which activities it can realistically engage in with the limited resources available. When not everyone pays dues, it may just be too expensive to send union newsletters to nonmembers, for example. So if you want to be in the loop as to the labor-management relations activity that affects every moment of your workplace life, that's another good reason to pony up your union dues.

Plus, It's the Fair Thing

Think about the relationship between a government and its citizens. Each of us approves of many of the decisions made on our behalf by our elected representatives but disagrees with others. Imagine the foolishness of trying to have a society where each person decided things based only on what was best for him or her individually. The fact is, we all benefit from understanding that the only practical way to live together is to have a group of people with common interests making group decisions. So each of us pays taxes, with the understanding that our pooled funds generally are used for the common good. In most cases, it's simply not practical to allow individuals to "opt out" of society's decisions. You, for example, may not have school-age children, but it would hardly be realistic for you to pay less taxes because you don't directly benefit from (or perhaps even do not approve of) spending on public education. One of this country's most distinguished Supreme Court justices, Oliver Wendell Holmes, put it succinctly: "Taxes are the price of civilization." Or, some of your neighbors may not think that the stop sign on the corner is really necessary. But you sure want them to obey it if your kid is trying to cross the street.

The relationship between a union and those it represents is the same as between a nation and its citizens. Unions exist because employees see that dealing with an employer only as individuals ultimately puts each of us in a weaker position. So we make the decision to work together as a group, and to have our elected union representatives implement decisions on behalf of the group. Will you agree with every single decision made by your union? Not a chance. But just the same, you and every other represented employee in your workplace benefits overall from the group decisions and actions. You may have thought in the last round of bargaining, for example, that the union should have pushed harder to improve the health benefits package. But the negotiated increase in wages that was won instead translated into more money in your paycheck.

So, just as with taxes, fairness dictates that everyone pays their rightful share of union dues. Everyone benefits from many of the uses to which our dues money is put, and is not pleased with some other uses. That's the nature of being a part of any group, be it your community association, your sports league, or your labor union.

The Law and Union Membership

What are your obligations of union membership and payment of dues? These days, thanks to a decision by the U.S. Supreme Court that turned decades of labor law upside down, those obligations are very different depending on whether you're a private sector employee covered by the National Labor Relations Act or a public sector worker. But before discussing what The Law says, here's a rundown of some of the basic principles of union membership and dues.

Private Sector: Union Shop/ Agency Shop

In some states, there's the possibility of workplaces where new employees are required to pay toward what's needed for the union to do its work. Such a "union security" provision in your contract may state that you are required to become a member of the union within a certain period of time after being hired, as a condition of keeping your job. Technically, what is being required in these cases is not full, dues-paying membership in the union but rather the regular payment of a defined amount of money, which can be less than full dues.

If you are covered by this kind of private sector union security arrangement, the law says you can choose not to pay the full dues amount. You may opt, instead, to pay what is called an "**agency fee**" or "**fair share**." You must pay one or the other, however; if you do not either join the union or make your fair share payment, you can lose your job.

> **Union Dues: Variations on the Theme**
>
> There are a number of modifications on dues obligations that are used in some unions. Here are a few of the most common ones:
>
> - **"Maintenance of membership"** is an arrangement in which all those who choose to become members of the union as of a certain date are required to maintain their memberships for a set period of time.
> - Some unions collect **"initiation fees,"** where those new to the trade pay a one-time "entry fee" into the union.
> - Under some collective bargaining agreements, new hires must successfully complete a probationary period before they acquire the full protections of the contract. Some unions start collecting dues only when an employee's probationary period is over.

For those who opt to pay only the reduced agency fee payment, the union usually is required to set the amount of that fee based on a calculation of what percentage of dues money is used directly for collective bargaining purposes. These "**chargeable**" expenses are those arising out of your union's representation activities: the costs of bargaining a contract, processing grievances and taking cases to arbitration, training union representatives, and the day-to-day expenses faced by the union in the course of promoting the interests of members of the bargaining unit. Unfortunately, court decisions often take a pretty narrow view of what makes up a union's "chargeable" items, that is, the ones that nonmembers are required to contribute to. Items such as political contributions, lobbying expenses, and social activities open only to union members cannot be included in the agency fee calculation. And the efforts by unions to win union representation in other workplaces may not be an allowable, chargeable amount as well. Despite the fact that these activities all help build union strength – and benefit everyone currently represented by the union – nonmembers are given the legal "right" to decline to pay their fair share.

Procedures dictated by law mandate that these fair share arrangements are carried out with fairness and transparency. For example, unions are required to have mechanisms in place for all of the following: notifying nonmembers annually of the calculation of the amount of agency fee required; disclosing financial information verified by an independent audit to back up that calculation; and allowing objecting nonmembers to pursue challenges to the calculations before an impartial decision maker.

Open Shop

Some unions operate in what are called **"right to work"** legal environments. These "RTW" arrangements apply to all public sector workers, and to private sector workers in some states.

The term "right to work" is intentionally misleading, since the "right" given by these laws is not in any sense the right to have a job. Rather, union-represented employees working in a "right to work" jurisdiction have the "right" to enjoy all of the benefits of union protection without paying a cent for it. As a matter of law, those individuals may not be required to make any financial contribution at all to the cost of that representation. Workplaces covered by this type of arrangement are referred to as "**open shops**." Loyal, dues-paying union members use a variety of terms to workers who refuse to pay their fair share for the union's work: "freeloaders" or "leeches" or "scab." (The word "scab" is also commonly used for workers who cross a picket line and go to work.) For the classic definition of a "scab," do a search for "Jack London scab" or go to: http://www.iamll1005.org/definition_of_a_scab.htm .

Closed Shop

The term "**closed shop**" refers to a workplace where you won't be hired unless you're already a member of the union. Such arrangements are illegal. They shouldn't be confused with union "**hiring halls**," though, a common practice in the private sector construction industry, where the union can legally serve as an exclusive source of referrals for job openings.

Objections to Union Membership

Since shouldering the full cost of the work done on behalf of you and others by your union is the right thing to do, in most instances there is no justification for refusing to join the union. Almost all those who refuse to make their fair financial contribution to their union either don't fully appreciate the collective nature of union representation, or are simply too cheap to pay full freight.

But there is a legally-recognized category that applies to a small number of employees who decline to make any payments at all to their union. The law does permit private sector employees whose religious beliefs preclude full union membership to opt out of what would otherwise be their financial obligations to the union. These religious beliefs are usually held by Seventh Day Adventists, though other groups, like the Amish, are also eligible. There are limits, though: one court, not surprisingly, rejected an argument that membership in the Ku Klux Klan was a legally protected "religion!" Religious "objectors" are allowed to make payments equivalent to union dues and fees to a designated nonreligious charity.

But most objections to paying union dues don't arise out of such decisions of conscience. A tremendous amount of costly and time-consuming litigation in defense of collecting dues has diverted substantial union resources from the job of representing members. Much of this has been sponsored by anti-union outfits such as the National Right to Work Committee, a group supported – no surprise here – by corporate interests. The huge drain on union resources caused by this litigation yields just what employers want: unions that are weakened because they lack the financial resources to fight on behalf of their members. So it's not hard to see why many in the union movement refer to the group sponsoring much of this litigation as the "National Right to Work *For Less* Committee."

National Right to Work: Seen and Unseen
High profile litigation and legislative work is only a part of what NRTW and its sibling organizational entities do. This huge operation has: 3,000 local chapters; a history including end runs around campaign finance laws and hiring private detectives to infiltrate the AFL-CIO and the NEA; and a headquarters operation in Springfield, VA big enough to have its own zip code!

The RTW crowd won a huge victory in the *Janus* case, where the U.S. Supreme Court ruled in 2018 that no public sector worker could be subject to paying their "fair share" of the costs of union representation. It had been settled law for over four decades that agency fee arrangements struck an appropriate balance between the rights of individual employees and the collective obligations of the union representing them. But with a new, employer-oriented majority on

What's Behind "Right to Work"?

While those advocating the "right to work" (RTW) use rhetoric that emphasizes "free choice" and "democratic" principles, the reality shows quite different motivations.

<u>Origins of RTW:</u> The man who started the first advocacy organization that used the term "right to work" in 1941 was Vance Muse of the Christian American Association. The other items on Muse's lifelong advocacy agenda shows where the right to work movement drew its inspiration. With funding from some of the nation's wealthiest industrialists and financiers, Muse waged vigorous public fights against women's suffrage, worked to defeat a constitutional amendment prohibiting child labor, and sought to repeal an eight-hour-day law for railroad workers. In 1944, one piece of his organization's literature warned that if a legislative effort to outlaw fair share payments failed, "white women and white men will be forced into organizations with black African apes...whom they will have to call 'brother' or lose their jobs."

Nowadays, there are lots of "institutes" and "centers" with high-sounding names that push RTW legislation and litigation and are similarly well-funded by some of the wealthiest corporate interests in America. The billionaire Koch brothers, for example, who have provided massive resources to the RTW effort, control the second largest privately-held company in the nation.

What's the real agenda of RTW? Fundamentally, it's to break the power of organized labor to fight for the interests of "the 99%" through political action. As we'll discuss in Chapter Eleven, although unions don't use dues to support political candidates, they do advocate on matters of public policy that affect working life. In the words of the National Federation of Independent Businesses, Inc.: "If unions are dealt a blow in the public sector, private sector businesses might see decreased pressure from pro-labor forces on issues ranging from the minimum wage to paid sick leave and other employee benefits." The anti-democratic (and anti-Democratic) effect of RTW was shown quite clearly by a recent study that found that right-to-work laws decrease the Democratic presidential vote share by 3.5 percent and depress overall turnout.

the Supreme Court, suddenly the U.S. Constitution meant the opposite of what it used to mean, and "The Law" did a 180 degree turn. So now – at least until the balance on the Supreme Court tilts once again in the direction of workers' rights – public sector employees who would rather not pay their fair share of the cost of union representation can justify this as part of their First Amendment free speech rights. The legal reasoning defies logic and is biased against labor, but there it is.

Dues: The Nuts and Bolt

There is tremendous variation from one union to another as to how dues amounts are set. And it is quite possible that the different components of your union dues (local, district or other intermediate body, and national/international) are calculated using different formulas and can be changed in different ways. The formula used for determining what your union dues are, and the mechanisms that are in place for making any changes, usually are found in the constitution and bylaws of the union at the various levels.

How Dues Amounts Are Determined

Sometimes dues are set at a flat dollar amount. If your union uses this approach, then you and all of your co-workers pay the identical amount in dues, regardless of the fact that your earnings may vary by quite a bit. This system has the advantages of simplicity and predictability of income flow for the union.

But some unions opt for a "progressive" dues structure, preferring a system where those who earn more pay more. Rather than setting dues at a dollar amount, these unions establish dues as a percentage of salary. When this method is used, everyone in the bargaining unit pays dues based on the same percentage. This has the effect of "socializing" the cost, since those who earn more pay more under such a formula.

Or your union may use a variation of this, with the amount of union dues determined by brackets of earnings. Under such a setup, everyone who makes within a certain range pays a set dollar amount in dues, everyone who makes somewhat more money pays a higher amount in dues, and so on.

Dues Increases

Your union dues may be set at a particular dollar amount, with any increases determined by whatever democratic procedures are in place for such decision making. The required processes sometimes are specified by law or by your union's

Unions Turn the Tables

There's no doubt that the anti-union forces that pushed the *Janus* case did so with the expectation that reducing the size of union treasuries would weaken unions. And in many instances, it has indeed become far more difficult for unions to provide high quality representation with limited financial resources.

But at least in some instances this employer plan has backfired. The loss of automatic income has given unions no choice but to work hard to convince each and every represented worker of the value of collective action and of the moral obligation to pay union dues. Examples abound of relatively weak unions with limited member support getting spurred to turn things around as a result of the Supreme Court's antiunion decision.

One good example of how laws designed to weaken unions can have the opposite effect is the case of unionized faculty at the University of Northern Iowa. After years of routine labor relations for public employees, the employer-friendly legislature drastically weakened the Iowa collective bargaining law, forbidding the negotiation of critically important items like health insurance, and eliminating members' ability to pay their union dues by means of payroll deduction. And before unions bargain a new contract, the new legislation required an election every time. In order to win the election, the union has to have a majority of those covered by the contract voting "yes," rather than just a majority of those who vote, which is how almost every other election in our country is decided.

At the time the new law was passed, less than half the faculty at UNI were paying their voluntary union dues. But the requirement for an up or down vote on continuing to have a union fired up the union supporters. They conducted an intensive campaign of one-on-one conversations, explaining to their colleagues that without the union, everyone would suffer. The result of the vote: 85% "yes"! So the union was able to move ahead with stronger support than it ever had before, and continue to tackle critical issues, like salary equity and job security for contingent faculty.

constitution or bylaws, and may include requiring a membership meeting where a secret ballot vote is taken, or holding a membership referendum. Sometimes it can be done by action of elected convention delegates.

Alternatively, a mechanism may be in place from the outset that automatically provides for annual or other periodic increases. For example, your union may have voted to establish a dollar amount for dues that is pegged to an hourly pay rate or a salary set by your collective bargaining agreement. So when an annual contractual raise kicks in, this automatically adjusts the dollar amount of the dues upward, as well.

If your dues are set by formula as a percentage of your earnings, then this automatically results in an increase in the dollar amount of your dues obligation as your earnings rise.

Initiation Fees and Assessments	Some unions require an initiation fee to be paid when you first join. Sometimes the amount is quite modest. In some industries, such as the building trades and the entertainment industry, it is not unusual to have initiation fees amount to a lot of money. Most unions have a system in place for obtaining an "**honorable withdrawal**" card if you do leave your union job for a period of time, so that you don't have to pay a new initiation fee if you come back to work in a unionized shop.

In addition to regular dues, your union local or national union may have an assessment of one sort or another, such as to fund strike benefits or new organizing projects.

The Mechanics of Paying Dues	In the early days of unions, the method by which workers paid their union dues was wonderfully straightforward and uncomplicated. On payday, the shop steward would come around and collect from each worker the nickel or dime that constituted union dues. This simple procedure clearly had advantages: like it or not, it compelled each union representative to have a one-on-one contact with each union member on a regular basis. But the drawbacks are easy to identify: especially in large workplaces, this was a tremendously time-consuming and cumbersome process.

These days, there are much easier – though more impersonal – ways that unions collect dues. Most workplaces have the option of a "**checkoff**" from your pay. Just as taxes are automatically deducted from your paycheck, so too are union dues. And just as you have to fill out a form when you start your job to trigger your payroll deduction of taxes, automatic payroll deduction of union dues most likely requires you to sign on the dotted line as well.

Some employees pay their union dues in other ways. You may, for example, simply write a check, either every payday, monthly, or even annually. Or, you may be able to authorize automatic payment from your bank account, your credit union, or by credit card.

Be aware that the amount of your union dues may qualify as a tax deduction. As they say, consult your tax adviser. . . .

THE UNION'S

responsibility

TO ITS MEMBERS

We've discussed the union's *right* to speak collectively for all in the bargaining unit – the concept of exclusive representation. Now let's take a look at the other side of the coin: the union's *obligation* to represent the interests of each individual in the unit. This requirement that the union advocates for the interests of each and every person in the bargaining unit is called "**the duty of fair representation**," **or "DFR."**

The Duty of Fair Representation

There are no hard and fast rules for what the union must do to live up to its duty of fair representation. There isn't even a precise definition of what that obligation consists of. When the United States Supreme Court and the National Labor Relations Board have wrestled with the meaning and extent of this obligation over the years, they have described it in such ways as "an honest effort to serve the interest of all . . . without hostility to any" and the right of bargaining unit members to be free from "unfair or irrelevant or insidious treatment" by their union representatives. The catch phrase most often used is that unions breach their obligation when they engage in actions that are "arbitrary, discriminatory or in bad faith." For example, a union steward cannot refuse to help a worker with a grievance just because of a personal dislike for that worker.

As a practical matter, the union obligation to represent the interests of all unit members fairly does not translate into a legal obligation always to speak for each individual member, nor does it require a union to be flawless in performing its representation duties. Let's take a look at each of these.

Balancing Different Interests

When a given issue arises, different individuals or groups within the bargaining unit may have different and even conflicting stakes in possible outcomes. For example, in contract negotiations the union might choose to push for raises calculated as a percentage of salary or it might seek raises as a flat dollar amount. The first formula puts more money in the pockets of those who already earn more, while the second ends up providing a greater percentage salary increase to lower-paid employees. There may be lots of good policy arguments for and against each of these alternatives, but in the end, whatever decision is made is going to be better financially for one group and not as good for the other. Since there's no way around this, the union is obligated only to act fairly in how it decides which direction to go, not to somehow come up with a magical solution that benefits everyone equally.

Perfection Not Required

No union has ever been legally required to have an impossible-to-achieve record of being flawless in the performance of its duties. Some legal decisions, though, have imposed a pretty demanding standard on unions. For example, suppose that your workplace is flooded by grievances and that your steward misplaces some paperwork and fails to process your grievance within the required timeframes. Or suppose that your steward fails to return a call or respond to an email inquiring about the status of your grievance. As regrettable as such oversights are, some jurisdictions now find that such occasional slipups constituting "mere negligence" – may be enough to violate the union's duty of fair representation. How strict the law is in this regard will depend on the specifics of the law that covers your union's jurisdiction, whether you are in the private sector or in a state or city with collective bargaining rights.

In all jurisdictions, it's clear that the union doesn't just have a blank check to decide how capably and fairly it will carry out its duties. For example, if the reason that your grievance was not processed in a timely way by the union was because of some personal grudge against you, you certainly would have a strong legal claim that the union therefore violated its DFR. Or if a particular steward (or your local union in general) has a pattern of failing to process grievances competently, that as well would add up to a strong claim of a breach of the duty of fair representation.

The examples given above are by far the most common situations in which allegations arise that the union has breached its DFR. With respect to the grievance/arbitration procedure, you may feel that a grievance you wish to pursue is not handled properly, or you may take issue with the union's decision not to take a particular grievance all the way to arbitration. Or you may believe the union acted improperly by not deciding even to initiate a grievance on your behalf. But the question of a violation of the DFR will turn on the facts in each case. It may be that the union didn't think that your case was winnable because the contract language wasn't clear enough to support your claim, or because it would be too difficult to prove the necessary facts to win the case. So long as the union investigated any conflicting claims before it made a good faith decision not to pursue the grievance, it has acted lawfully.

On the contract bargaining front, arriving at an agreement with the employer ultimately depends on reaching a series of mutually acceptable compromises. So the bargaining process, by its nature, results in individual bargaining unit members having different degrees of satisfaction with the final agreement. Even coming up with the union's initial bargaining proposals involves weighing and balancing sometimes competing interests of different groups within the union membership. Once again, as long as the union's motivation in making those necessary tradeoffs isn't improper there's no violation of the DFR.

A union's responsibilities cover a wide range of matters, so there are other situations as well in which the DFR may be an issue. For example, if you exercise what's known as your Weingarten right to have a union representative present when you're being questioned by the employer (discussed in Chapter 10) you have the right to expect a certain level of competence on the part of the representative your union provides. Or if you consult the union about a health and safety concern, or about another aspect of workplace rights, you similarly are entitled to a reasonable effort on the part of the union to give you guidance.

If Your Rights May Have Been Violated

If you believe that your union has not lived up to its duty of fair representation, or even if you just have some questions or concerns about the quality of the representation provided, your first step is to sort out exactly what happened and why. It's simply not fair to your co-workers who have stepped forward to do the union's work to react by making accusations without first checking out the facts. So approach your steward, or anyone else who had responsibility for the action you are unhappy about, state your concerns, and try to listen with an open mind to whatever explanations are offered. Just as with dealing with an employer representative, you may want to be cautious and have a third party present for such a discussion.

Evaluate the explanation that is offered. Try to be objective. You may not like the fact that the union didn't go to bat for you. But try to take a step back and see whether the decision that was made might have been a reasonable and fair one under the circumstances, one attempting to balance the different needs and interests of different individuals.

If you are not satisfied with the explanation that you have been given, you may well have a number of options. There may be an internal union procedure set up so that union members can air complaints about actions the union has taken. Some unions have quite elaborate mechanisms, including neutral, outside parties who come in and review the circumstances. Alternatively, there may be formal legal action you can take, including filing an unfair labor practice charge or a lawsuit alleging a violation of the duty of fair representation. You may well need to consult with an attorney or with a worker advocacy group, to sort out what your legal rights are.

Dig Deeper for Solutions? But before choosing to assert any individual legal rights you may have regarding your union, give some thought to analyzing the underlying problem. If you were the unfortunate victim of a single incompetent steward, this may not be the union's "fault" in any realistic sense. So to be fair to the union as a whole, you might want to decline to press any legal claim you might have. On the other hand, the treatment by the union that you are unhappy about may be part of a much larger problem that the union has. It may be that the top leadership is not fairly taking into account the legitimate interests of large groups of members, or falls so short in its leadership ability that the entire organization has become weak and ineffective. If this is the case, the solution to the problem is larger than whatever you might hope to achieve in pursuing an individual duty of fair representation legal claim. What is needed may be a change in the elected leadership, or at least for those individuals to receive a wake-up call. If this is the situation that your local is in, then you and your or co-workers should give some thought to how to exercise your democratic rights as union members to improve the union. You'll want to start with dialog, trying to persuade your union brothers and sisters that a change in direction is needed. But if more forceful action is needed, you've got the legal right to pursue it. Information on exercising these rights is found in the next section, Internal Union Rights.

Alternate Relief?

Finally, don't lose sight of the fact that you may have the ability to pursue independently whatever your underlying complaint was, even if the union hasn't acted on your behalf. For example, if the union elected not to pursue a grievance in which you alleged unlawful discrimination, you may well have the right to go to a state or federal agency, or to a court, to pursue your discrimination claim on your own. Since the union will not be involved, you will need to weigh any financial costs associated with pursuing such a legal action unassisted.

Internal Union Rights

As individual Americans we have a host of legal rights that attempt to guarantee our participation in a democratic society. These include free speech rights, the right to obtain information about what our elected leaders and government do in our name, and the right to vote. Let's take a look at the rights that you have as a union member to participate in the democratic workings of your collective bargaining representative.

The law setting forth your legal rights to participate in your union generally grows out of a federal statute passed in 1959, known as the **Landrum-Griffin Act**. Specifically, the **Labor Management Reporting and Disclosure Act (LMRDA)**, administered by the U.S. Department of Labor, covers unions with members in the private sector. If your union represents both public and private sector workers, this law may also apply to you, as it will if you are a postal service employee. While this discussion will center on the LMRDA, the concepts and rights contained in that statute are generally quite similar to those that apply to public sector union members as well.

Speaking Up, at Union Meetings and Elsewhere

As a union member, you enjoy a broad set of rights similar in many ways to the rights found in the First Amendment to the U.S. Constitution. The LMRDA's "Bill of Rights of Members of Labor Organizations" contains an "equal rights" provision, guaranteeing all union members in good standing the right to nominate candidates for union office, to vote in union elections, and to attend and participate in union meetings. That federal law does not specifically require labor organizations to hold meetings. But it does say that when meetings are held you have the right to participate fully. Keep in mind that there's another source of rights you may have related to holding union meetings, electing officers, and voting on dues increases in new contract agreements: your union's constitution and bylaws. So even though the law may not require your union to hold a meeting, your local's constitution and bylaws probably will contain such a provision. Another reason to take the time to read the bylaws once you become a union member.

The labor "Bill of Rights" also guarantees "freedom of speech and assembly." The law says that unions are allowed to have "reasonable rules" regarding how it runs its affairs. But you, the union member, have a guaranteed right to have and to express your viewpoints on the union and those who lead and participate in it, even if those viewpoints are critical or negative ones.

Union Elections

While the decision whether to hold meetings may be left to the discretion of a union, specific legal rules apply to holding an election for union officers and conducting a referendum on dues increases or other financial assessments of members. At least for unions directly covered by the LMRDA and for unions in the federal sector, there are specific requirements dealing with the frequency of elections for union officers at all the various levels of a union, and how those elections must be conducted. These detailed requirements cover your right to run for union office, the types of balloting – on the jobsite, by mail, electronically and so forth – and much else. You can read through the soup to nuts explanation of all the legal requirements that apply to these union elections on line at the website for the federal Department of Labor, at https://www.dol.gov/olms/regs/compliance/localelec/localelec.htm. At the local level, your union must provide for election of officers by secret ballot, and it must do so no less frequently than every three years. For national-level officers, there's a five year election rule. Only members in good standing have the right to vote.

Union Financial Information

Whether under the LMRDA or similar public sector laws, unions generally are required to file various information reports with a government agency and to make the information available to their members. For private sector employees, these **Labor Management or "LM" Reports** are public information, easily available on line at https://www.dol.gov/olms/regs/compliance/localelec/localelec.htm. The LM-2 form is like a tax return. Unions file them annually, and these forms are worth tracking down if you wish to obtain detailed information as to your union's financial status, such as assets and liabilities, salaries and expenses of union officers and staff, and any loans the union may have granted to members or businesses. Smaller unions file an LM-3 of LM-4 form, which are simplified versions of the LM-2.

47

A word of caution if you're doing some research on your union's finances: stick with the official Department of Labor filings for the accurate information. There's an anti-union outfit running a website (UnionFacts.com) with information on union finances that doesn't always have a good track record for accuracy. The Washington Post "fact checker" once referred to a $3.5 million dollar ad it ran during the Super Bowl as relying on "a nonsense fact."

Protection and Enforcement

The LMRDA also protects your exercise of internal union rights by making it illegal for a union to "fine, suspend, expel, or otherwise discipline any of its members for exercising any right to which he is entitled." So a union can't discipline a member for expressing unpopular viewpoints, for forming an opposition caucus within the union, or for campaigning for candidates who are running against incumbent union officers.

In fact, legal cases have held that in the rough and tumble of union politics, unions cannot discipline members who make untrue statements about union officers. But keep in mind that there are limits, of course, to these rights you have within your union: the law will not, for example, protect you if you publicly call upon your co-workers to quit the union and join a rival union.

If a union does have justification for initiating a disciplinary action, it must provide certain due process protections such as written notice of the specific charges and a fair opportunity to respond to them, and it must follow the procedures that are in its own constitution and bylaws.

The LMRDA is enforced by the Department of Labor and the courts.

Trusteeships

Most unions at the national or state level have the authority under certain circumstances to impose what are known as "**trusteeships**" (sometimes called "**receiverships**" or "**administratorships**") on locals.

During the period of trusteeship, a union local loses control over its assets and the day-to-day running of union affairs. For as long as the trusteeship is in force, an individual appointed by the national union assumes this day-to-day authority. Periodic reports must be filed detailing the reason the trusteeship was imposed and reporting on all of the financial implications.

The law says that a union may be placed into trusteeship only for certain reasons, and whatever procedures are outlined in the union's constitution and bylaws must be followed.

Trusteeships often serve useful purposes in weeding out pockets of corruption in union locals, and in helping locals that are in trouble because of extreme fiscal mismanagement or political infighting get back on their feet. At the same time, there can be abuses of the authority to impose trusteeships, where a national union has tried to simply impose its will on a local.

In the unlikely event that your local is placed into trusteeship and you do not think that this action is in the best interest of the members, you have the right as an individual member to initiate a challenge. A complaint on your part can trigger an inquiry into whether proper grounds exist for placing your local in trusteeship and whether the necessary procedures were followed.

YOUR

union contract

GETTING THERE

Society functions under a set of laws passed by legislators. The workplace functions under a collective bargaining agreement negotiated by the union and the employer. Both serve the same purpose: to create binding rules on what is permitted and what is prohibited.

How does a contract get negotiated? Sometimes the law under which a particular union and employer operate sets out specific procedures for reaching a collective bargaining agreement. Or in the union contract itself, your union and employer may have agreed upon some rules for how the next contract is to be negotiated. Exactly how the bargaining process shapes up will be determined in large part by whether you are in the public or private sector, and by the ground rules or history of the parties in your industry or workplace. For example, in some industries – such as auto manufacturing or the U.S. Postal Service – national contracts are bargained, and sometimes only certain issues are then subject to negotiations at the local level. In others – at newspapers, for example, or your local police or fire department – every issue is worked out right there. The general process of getting a new contract looks pretty much the same, no matter what type of work you do, who employs you, or what union represents you.

The Bargaining Process

The formal bargaining process generally begins when the union presents its proposals (sometimes called "demands") at the negotiating table at a time and place agreed to by both sides. Either at that session or later on, the employer usually brings in proposals of its own. In most cases, it's the union that puts the bargaining issues on the table and sets the stage for the negotiations. But if the employer has been facing hard times or wants to make substantial changes because of new technology or outside pressures, it can be the employer that lays down its marker first

How does a union come up with what its bargaining agenda will be? The process the union goes through to figure out what proposals to present usually includes looking at:

- what the workforce's experience has shown is "broken" in the old contract, and what therefore needs to get "fixed" in the new one;

- how to balance the needs and expectations of various groups of employees represented by the union; for example, professional and clerical employees in the same bargaining unit, or day shift and night shift workers, or newer employees and those with greater seniority, which will sometimes be quite different or even in conflict;

- what the union itself needs so it can function as an effective advocate for its members, like getting an office on-site or time off for union stewards so they can process grievances;

- the reality of what's happening in your and other workplaces in your sector, and in the labor economy climate in general. For example, is inflation so high that it's reasonable to expect substantial cost of living raises? Are health care costs increasing so fast that everyone is either paying more or seeing benefits get trimmed? Is your employer facing hard times, or is it flush with cash? These are all factors that play into union negotiations.

Surveying the Members

Unions begin preparations for bargaining by educating their members about how and when bargaining will take place and what the key issues may be. To find out what's on your mind, your union may hold meetings, sometimes called "contract proposal meetings," to ask you and your co-workers directly what problems you'd like your negotiators to tackle in bargaining. Very often some sort of written or electronic survey is distributed to determine what the top priorities should be and how important each one is in the members' eyes. This communication is a two-way street: savvy union negotiators use questionnaires or newsletters early on not only to gather information but also to educate members on the issues that probably will be major areas of labor-management conflict in bargaining. Used this way, a bargaining survey is a tool to begin to build unity.

Whether it's a questionnaire or a workplace meeting, this first stage is your opportunity to weigh in on the things in your working life that you'd like to see changed through bargaining. At the beginning and then throughout the bargaining process, if your steward, bargaining committee members and other union leaders need to know what you and your co-workers really want. In the words of the baseball great Yogi Berra, "If you don't know where you're going, you might not get there."

Selecting the Bargaining Team

There's no "one size fits all" for bargaining committees, since the size and makeup of each workplace is different. Bargaining a contract requires a tremendous amount of time and effort, in both face-to-face negotiations and in each side doing separate preparation and research. Teams need to be small enough to get the work done efficiently. But it also makes sense for a union bargaining team to be large enough to include people with a close understanding of the needs of the various types of people in the bargaining unit. Whether the differences are those of day and night workers, skilled and unskilled, male and female, different races or cultural groups, or anything else, the union needs some way of making sure that the bargaining team can speak forcefully and accurately for all members.

By the way, don't assume that just because you've never bargained a contract before, it's out of the question that you could be included on the bargaining team. It's a smart move for unions to put a couple of less experienced people at the bargaining table, as a way of doing on the job training for the next generation of negotiators. And newer members on a negotiating team can bring a fresh perspective that is helpful to the older hands. If you do become a member of the bargaining team, that might be by being elected or appointed, depending on how your union handles this. No matter your route to the bargaining team, be prepared for an intensive work effort, likely lasting for months or even longer. It's a big responsibility, involving not only hours and hours sitting across from management, but also meeting with your team members and with the union leadership to hammer out your next moves at the table. People at your job site will be looking to you for information. You may also need to miss work or other functions to attend bargaining sessions. But if you've got the commitment and the inclination, it's one of the most important and rewarding union activities you can take on.

There are other ways, too, that you can be involved in the bargaining process. Think about asking to work on a union bargaining subcommittee that will have the job of researching the issues or digging up facts to respond to what the employer's pushing for. Or, if your union sets things up this way, you could volunteer to be a special bargaining representative for your work area. Your job then is to help the union negotiators by distributing information on what's happening at the table through handing out flyers or holding small worksite meetings, and to function as the union's "eyes and ears" on the shop floor, so that the union bargaining team can keep alert to what the members are thinking. Or you may be able to serve on a special bargaining council, usually a pretty large group set up so that representatives from each work area advise the bargaining team throughout negotiations.

Face-to-Face Negotiations

The bargaining process always includes face-to-face sessions, conducted in a fairly formal way. Notes are taken so the parties will have a record of what was said if a dispute later comes up over what did or didn't happen during the talks. Depending on the type of union and the type and size of the bargaining unit, negotiations for the union will be done either by a single spokesperson or by individuals on the bargaining team, with each addressing a specific area of concern. The bargainers present proposals and the facts, figures and arguments that justify them. Since each side has proposals and counterproposals of its own, the sessions also include asking questions about what the other side is proposing and why, and debating the facts and arguments. Especially when the issues being addressed are fairly technical – like the calculation of retirement benefits, or the costs of a health care plan – there may well be experts brought in to lead the discussion for each side.

Bargaining is a process of give and take, with both sides trying to take as much as they can and give as little as possible. Throughout negotiations, each party meets in between sessions and holds caucuses (team-only meetings) during the middle of bargaining sessions. This time is used by each side to sort through which of its proposals it needs to keep pushing for, and which of the other side's it may be willing to agree to. Issue by issue, the parties explore areas of acceptable compromise to see where agreement can be reached. As the parties reach agreement on language for articles in the contract, these "**tentative agreements**" are set aside until the rest of the contract is in place.

As the bargaining process goes on, the union may report back to the membership what items the parties have agreed to and where the remaining conflicts are. Sometimes members will be allowed and even encouraged by the union to sit in on bargaining sessions. If you can, take the opportunity to see firsthand how the union presents the employees' point of view and how the employer lays out its agenda. It can be a real eye opener to witness the employer's representatives continually saying "no" to things you know are totally reasonable. It also sends a useful message to the employer when they see union members willing to take the time to show up and visibly support their bargaining team.

Bargaining a contract from start to finish can take quite a bit of time. Sometimes bargaining is not wrapped up by the time the old contract has expired. When that happens, one of two things takes place: either the parties keep bargaining or there is a showdown then and there. In a moment we'll look at what exactly this "showdown" may consist of, based on the particular circumstances of your bargaining. But depending on a number of legal factors and what the parties may have worked out if bargaining continues past the expiration date of the old contract, the terms of the old contract may well remain in effect. So even though in some ways you're in between contracts, your employer still has to do what the old contract required.

Concluding an Agreement

Even when the parties reach agreement at the table on all items, it's usually not a done deal yet. Others often must approve these tentative agreements before they are signed, sealed and delivered. On the employer side, sometimes a board of directors or higher-ups in the organization will have to give final approval, or the legislature will have to agree to fund a public sector contract wage or benefit package. On our side, either the union bylaws or the practice of the union usually provides for member "**ratification**" of the agreement – a vote to accept or reject. Keep in mind, though, that there are some situations when you won't get to vote approval or disapproval of a contract; for example, if a settlement ultimately is handed down by an outside arbitrator, as described below.

Either at a union meeting or through printed or electronic material, you should be provided a full opportunity to educate yourself on the provisions of the tentative agreement that you're being asked to vote on. Typically, the bargaining team or the union leadership will make a recommendation on whether the contract should be voted up or down. Sometimes union leaders and the negotiating committee will be at polling sites to answer any specific questions on the agreement. Most of the time, the recommendation on ratification is affirmative. But your union leaders may well recommend a "no" vote on the contract, as a tactic or if the negotiating team is not making enough progress towards an acceptable deal. A vote by the rank and file to reject a tentative contract agreement and to send the union negotiators back to the bargaining table is sometimes an effective way of showing the employer's negotiators that what's been offered just isn't enough to settle the contract.

Actual voting on a contract can take place through a mail or electronic ballot or at a union meeting where the vote may be by either open or secret ballot. Almost always, only dues-paying members of the union get to vote on accepting or rejecting the contract. And just as in elections for U.S. president or for legislative representatives, the outcome is determined by those who take the time and trouble to vote. When you choose not to cast a vote in the democratic process of contract ratification, you are letting others decide for you what law of the workplace you will live under.

When you are faced with the often difficult decision of whether to ratify a tentative agreement on a new contract, keep in mind that this vote is different from votes you cast in other parts of your life. In state and national elections, we vote to elect someone else to do a job for us. In voting on a collective bargaining agreement, our vote obligates *us* to do certain things. We usually don't have the luxury of just voting "no" and then figuring that someone else will do what's needed to make things better. Chances are, the reason the bargaining team came back to the

It's Not Just "the Union Contract"

Don't be misled by the shorthand term "union contract." Understandably, people call it that because the union negotiates it. But every contract is a deal struck by two parties and is binding on both. In the case of a collective bargaining agreement, this means that your employer and your union have gone through a process of give and take. At the end they reached an agreement under which both sides have rights and obligations. So it's not really just the "union contract," it's the "union and employer" contract, since both sides have to live by its terms.

Understand, too, that a union contract is fundamentally different from other contracts you're used to, say a contract to buy a house or a car. In such private contracts, we're unlikely to accept terms we don't like. If the price the dealer asks for the car is too high, we simply don't sign a contract to buy it at that price, and we look around for a better deal or just decide to do without a new car for the time being. But the terms of a collective bargaining agreement reflect the relative power between the union and the employer. You and your union may not be pleased with some of the provisions in a contract settlement, but you may not have the power to reject a deal with those terms. A bad contract provision can't simply be sent back to the kitchen like an undercooked steak in a restaurant. Sometimes wisdom is the better part of valor, and the smart move is to take the best deal you can get this time and organize more effectively to win more in the next round of bargaining. Always remember this: without fail, *the stronger the union, the stronger the union contract.*

membership with what they did was because they got the best deal that seemed possible under the circumstances. So you usually will need to think of your vote to reject a tentative contract agreement as being a vote to change those circumstances: to get personally involved, so that the union will then have the extra clout needed to get a better settlement than what you just turned down.

If a contract is ratified, sometimes it takes a little while for the final language to get tidied up and the new contract to be in place. Once it's finalized, you should check out the terms for yourself, exercising your legal right to receive or examine the collective bargaining agreement that covers your job, so you can know your workplace rights.

If a contract is voted down by the members, what next? Sometimes, the two sides will return to the bargaining table and try again to work out an acceptable deal. But sometimes they won't go back to negotiating, and a deadlock results.

What Happens If the Parties Deadlock?

Sometimes at the table the answer to the question "do you want to make a deal?" stays stuck at "no." When the two sides can't reach agreement at the bargaining table on all the terms of a new contract, a variety of mechanisms may kick in to determine the outcome, depending on the law that applies to your jurisdiction.

• In many cases, the parties call in a "**mediator**." That's a neutral labor professional who works with both sides to try to find areas of acceptable compromise. The mediator has no authority to impose a resolution of the issues the parties disagree on. But a skillful mediator is sometimes able to push one side or the other to be willing to compromise, or may come up with a creative alternative solution to a thorny issue that both parties can then agree to.

• Or a professional "**factfinder**" or "**arbitrator**" may take evidence and issue a report on what the final contract should contain. Sometimes this is advisory, sometimes it's binding.

• If common ground can't be found, the union may be able to call a strike in the hope that the employer's loss of production or ability to provide services to customers will force a softening of its bargaining position. Since the stakes are high when workers go on strike, no union takes this option lightly. There's always substantial discussion about whether a strike is a realistic way for the union to win, and there's a vote by the membership to authorize a strike, if needed, in advance of any walkout actually taking place.

• On the employer side of the equation, it may have a variety of ways to turn up the heat. If a bunch of legal hoops are jumped through, there may be a right to simply unilaterally impose the specific terms of the employer's "**last, best offer**"

58

that the parties have reached deadlock on. Or a hard line company might close the facility and "**lock out**" the workers, thereby cutting off pay and benefits for the duration.

Disputes that get contentious enough that a strike or lockout occurs or is even a real possibility usually are resolved when one side or the other feels pressured enough to make whatever additional compromises are needed to result in an agreement.

What Happens in a Strike?

Private sector workers and many public employees have the right to strike. Strikes are called either to get a first contract for a newly unionized workplace or to pressure the employer to agree to a more favorable settlement after a contract expires. (There are instances, although rare, where unions can use strikes while a contract is still in effect.) Going out on strike is generally the last resort for a union. To reduce hardship there is usually provided (at least partial) strike pay, so that strikers can keep paying their bills while they stand firm. Some unions offer members in need short term loans to ease the short-term economic impact. And you may live in a state where workers are eligible to collect unemployment compensation while they are out on strike. At the conclusion of a strike, the settlement might or might not include a provision that the workers will be able to make up the lost pay from the employer.

Strikes are riskier than they used to be. In the past, it was pretty much par for the course that if there was no agreement on a new contract, at midnight when the old contract expired the union brought pressure to bear by simply "stopping production." That is, the members stopped working. As a practical matter, in a manufacturing setting this meant simply preventing Widget Company from continuing its widget production. In a service setting, the workers would no longer provide services to customers or to the public.

Over the years, private sector companies and public employers have become much more aggressive in their responses to strikes. Both have tried more and more often to get rid of strikers and do what they can to continue conducting business as usual. Sometimes it's clear that the employer actually wants a strike, because it thinks that it can break the union's will that way. So employers will force a strike by offering terms at the table that they know the union can never accept, and then rely on using temporary replacement workers – or even permanent replacements – to continue business operations without the union workers.

Changing Technology => Changing Terrain for Labor-Management Fights

As effective as strikes still can prove to be, in some industries changing technology has meant that it is increasingly difficult for unions simply to stop production in this way.

In a turning point in the 1970's, The Washington Post led the way into a new era of confrontational labor relations when it got around solid union picket lines outside its building by using helicopter pickups on its roof. And now that computer technology has made telecommuting widespread, companies can "produce" their product without employees on site, especially when the striking unionized workers already are doing their jobs remotely. When this is the setup of the workplace, as a practical matter setting up a physical picket line will likely be less effective in putting pressure on the employer.

Two Types of Strikes

The law in the private sector divides strikes into two categories. The first is "**economic strikes**" when unions go out to win a contract with more money and better working conditions. With respect to job rights in this context, the law makes a distinction that perhaps only a lawyer can fully appreciate: a company may not legally fire striking workers, but it may lawfully "**permanently replace**" them. (Many a "permanently replaced" worker has felt very much fired.) So unless the union can negotiate a wholesale return to work at the end of the strike, each striker is placed on a waiting list for future job vacancies as they arise. Keep in mind that regardless of what the law may permit an employer to do, in the end, the solidarity of the workers and the strength of the union can make it impossible for the employer to refuse to take all the union workers back.

The second strike category is what are known as "**unfair labor practice strikes**." These are strikes that are triggered not by economic or contract demands of the union but by a union protest over certain unlawful actions taken by the company. "Unfair labor practices" are violations of a bargaining law, and include such actions as firing a worker for union activism or for protesting health and safety violations. In unfair labor practice strikes, a company is permitted to hire substitute workers, but only on a temporary basis. Even if the union does not win the strike, once the union declares that the workers are ready to go back to their jobs, the company must take them back.

For public employee unions who face a deadlock at the bargaining table, often the law requires the services of a neutral third party – a mediator, factfinder or arbitrator. Some public employees ultimately have the legal right to strike, but many don't have that right. Sometimes this is because the bargaining law in that state doesn't permit any public workers at all to strike, and sometimes it's because a particular group of workers (like police or fire fighters) are in a category where the law says it would be too disruptive to allow strikes. But the fact is, some unions that don't have the legally-protected right to strike still do so anyway, and they're strong enough to get away with it.

The Real Power: Away from the Table

Wouldn't the world be a wonderful place if those with better arguments, and the facts and what's morally right on their side, always won out? But like much else in life, the outcome of contract negotiations is determined in large part simply by who has more power. Each side constantly evaluates during bargaining whether it can hold firm in its positions and wait for the other side to back down, or whether it must compromise if it wants to reach agreement. These decisions always are based on an assessment of how much each side can successfully exert pressure on the other if agreement is not reached.

Because of these power dynamics, effective union negotiators don't conceive of bargaining as taking place in a vacuum. Throughout negotiations, unions that understand the big picture look for ways to demonstrate that the members stand strong behind their bargaining team. If an employer gets the message that the small group of union negotiators it's dealing with face to face is in fact speaking for large numbers of bargaining unit members, that creates pressure for the employer to give the union what it wants. Most important, the employer must come to believe that if issues aren't successfully resolved at the table, the members won't take the employer's "no" for an answer.

What this means is that if you want a good contract, you and your union may well not have the luxury of simply sending dedicated and skilled union negotiators off to deal with the employer and then waiting until they come back with a string of victories. Having a bargaining team consisting of folks with the needed expertise is necessary, but not sufficient, to win a solid contract. Actions outside of the bargaining room are almost always essential to get what's needed inside that room.

Contract Campaigns

As your negotiating team goes through the process of exchanging proposals with the employer, arguing them out, and seeing where acceptable resolutions can be found, you may be called upon to step forward and play a different type of role in the bargaining process. Your union may ask you and your co-workers to let the employer and perhaps also the public know in a variety of ways that the voice of the union negotiators is also your voice.

In the pre-digital age, the actions called for were usually quite straightforward: members signed petitions supporting a contract demand or wore a certain color T-shirt on a "solidarity day" scheduled by the union. Nowadays, union leaders and members themselves use the newer forms of communication made possible by changing technology to get the word out, to coworkers and to the public, about what's holding up a contract settlement. A high degree of member activity on social media can be one way of demonstrating to the employer that the union's positions at the bargaining table enjoy broad support among the membership, and the community. Some examples:

• Union members and their supporters may be asked to change their profile picture on social media to a graphic designed by the union to highlight a particular campaign.
• Support for a union fight can be demonstrated to everyone an individual has contact with by adding a tagline to an email signature block.
• Photos or videos of people holding a sign showing support for the union fight can be posted on Facebook, Instagram, Snap Chat or other social media sites.

•   Since Twitter is mostly used as a news outlet and a breeding ground for reporters and journalists, "Twitter storms" can be organized by the union to bring awareness to campaigns. (In a Twitter storm, supporters are asked to send a sample tweet at the same time on the same day to a specific target to demonstrate solidarity with the union.)

One word of caution on wide-open digital communication, though: usually the union leadership has carefully thought through what the best public message is to gain support for the union negotiators. So think twice about making individual comments on line that might pull things in a different direction, or signal to the employer that there's division within the union ranks.

Two more words of caution are needed regarding information about union activities that you receive on line or through social media. First, there are anti-union outfits that put out information that is misleading at best, and quite often outright untrue. They exaggerate horror stories about unions, and try to drive a wedge between members and their unions. For example, they'll list "compensation" of union leaders or staff, which folds in fringe benefits (like health insurance, retirement, and so on) or expenses that the union has reimbursed these folks for job-related travel they've done. This creates the impression of union "fat cats"

That Certain Flash...

One particular use of digital communication to demonstrate public support shows the role that fun can play in public support campaigns. At a number of low wage businesses – Walmart, McDonald's and the like – flash mobs have been organized. A flash mob is a group of people who gather in a public place unannounced, do a quick action, usually a choreographed dance, and then disperse. These flash mobs build the workers' fight in two ways: they gum up the employer's operations for a short time, and they also entertain customers as they educate them. Plus, someone's inevitably filming the flash mob action, and posting it on social media afterwards to further spread the word.

Yes, goin' to have some fun can be an effective union weapon!

living large on your dues dollars, though these folks are actually just making a reasonable living. Or they'll tell the story of companies being driven into bankruptcy by greedy unions, with all the workers losing their jobs. (For the record, it is *not* true that "Unions Killed Twinkies"!)

Second, some of the information badmouthing unions is just plain false. Bottom line, it's easier than it should be for anyone (or any foreign government) to set up fake accounts and post made-up information to mislead people. So, reader beware!

As things heat up in bargaining, increasingly assertive actions may be called for. There may be rallies on or off the worksite or an informational picket before or after work at the employer's premises. Eventually the union may feel the need to have the members withhold their labor, either for a short period of time or in a full-blown strike. A pressure campaign against the employer that is fought on many fronts – a "**contract campaign**" – has been the key to union victory in many a contract fight.

Corporate Campaigns

64

Unions use "**corporate campaigns**" as another way to wage a broader fight outside the bargaining room. These fights on a second front can supply the leverage to force an employer to give in to the union's bargaining demands.

In a way, the end game in the bargaining process used to be pretty straightforward. If the parties didn't see eye to eye at the table, then economic pressure was brought to bear: either the union would strike or the employer would lock out the workers. The terms of the eventual contract settlement would be determined by how much each side felt pain in the pocketbook.

But recent years have brought us negative developments in the law, shifts in the American (and world) economy, and the new technology that sometimes takes control of production out of the workers' hands. These have changed the union view of strikes. Now, unions often conclude that a strike is a last resort, used only if there is no other effective weapon in their arsenal.

So changing times and power relationships have launched the corporate campaign as a new form of union action.

In a corporate campaign, rather than just calling a strike, the union analyzes where the employer's weaknesses lie, and that's where it brings pressure to bear. A few examples:

• A hospital's business depends on how much confidence patients and potential patients have in its services; so the union may take out ads or run radio spots to publicize how understaffing affects the quality of care provided. The same understaffing argument is often made by unions representing educators. As classroom size increases, the quality of education suffers.

• An employer may rely heavily on consumers viewing it as a good "corporate citizen," and may therefore be nervous about having its image tarnished; one newspaper union, for example, made a public point in bargaining of dramatizing that part-time workers (who received low wages and no company benefits) were forced to make ends meet by getting food stamps.

• A public agency needs continual funding from the legislature, so the union may collect and disclose examples of wasteful expenditures of taxpayer dollars by the agency.

In a given situation, creative pressure tactics may prove to be as effective, or 65 even more effective than a traditional strike. This is especially true when solidarity by other unions, community groups, or the general public can be used to pressure the employer. If your union decides to go this route, you may be an essential part of the plan: collecting information about what's going on in the workplace, for example, or publicizing in the community information that the union has dug up on the employer.

The Legal Framework for Negotiations

Bargaining laws seldom dictate the specifics of what the parties must agree to in the course of negotiations. But they do set forth a framework for bargaining. Here are some of the basic legal principles.

<u>Duty to bargain in good faith.</u> While laws may not force either side to agree to any particular proposal, they do require negotiators to approach bargaining with "a sincere resolve" to reach agreement. Labor boards and judges that oversee bargaining won't stand in the way of negotiators taking firm positions and

aggressively trying to get the other side to give at the table. But in the eyes of the law, it's not enough to just go through the motions of bargaining. Each party must be willing to meet with the other at reasonable times and places, to be reasonably flexible in modifying positions, and to demonstrate in other ways that it is genuinely trying to reach agreement.

<u>Subjects of bargaining.</u> Depending on the law covering your type of workplace, subjects of bargaining may be:

- **"Mandatory,"** meaning that the parties *must* bargain over them if either side wants to. The covered topics are those dealing with "wages, hours, and other terms and conditions of employment," likely including health plans, pensions, leave policies, and so on.

- **"Permissive"** (or **"nonmandatory"**), meaning that either side has the right to decide for itself whether or not it is willing to bargain over that subject. Examples might be a proposal to change which employees are covered by the collective bargaining agreement, or one that addresses health and welfare or pension plans for retirees.

- **"Non-negotiable"** or illegal, meaning that the collective bargaining agreement cannot address that topic at all. The parties to a contract, for example, couldn't legally bargain over a contract provision that would be in violation of a law prohibiting discrimination.

<u>The right to information.</u> This is part of the framework of bargaining. In basic terms, the law says that if one party needs information to address issues to be discussed in negotiations, the other side must turn over that information. (This right, by the way, also applies to information that's needed during the life of a contract to enforce its terms, such as when a union needs to get a look at employer records to pursue a grievance.)

Interest-Based Bargaining

Like most everything else in society, the dynamics of the labor relations process transform over the years. The adversarial way that bargaining historically has been conducted has not been replaced, by any means. But one newer model that is sometimes used is worth looking at.

Starting from some very different assumptions than those that form the basis of traditional negotiations, a relatively recent style of bargaining seeks to enable parties to reach agreement by using a new set of procedures. This form of negotiation goes by several different names: **interest-based bargaining**, **mutual-gains bargaining**, or sometimes **win-win**.

The standard style of bargaining strongly resembles a game of poker. In a card game, it is understood by all that you are expected to hold your cards close to the vest; you've got no ethical or other obligation to let any of the other players know, in effect, where your strengths and weaknesses lie. In fact, the unwritten rules by which the game is played make it acceptable deliberately to mislead the other players by using such tactics as bluffing. Similar unspoken ground rules also dictate the behavior of the parties in negotiations. Outright lying is not okay. But it's all in the (collective bargaining) game that a good deal of puffery and posturing is understood to be part of the way the game is played.

Negotiators in a standard bargaining relationship also need to possess many of the skills of good chess players. A skillful negotiator must think ahead to make the series of decisions at a bargaining table about what items to trade off, and when to do so. What will the other side's response be if I make this possible statement or take that possible action? And what options will those responses then leave me? This is the same type of strategizing that goes into a good game of chess: thinking ahead by a number of moves if you can.

As the standard bargaining process draws to a close, the dynamic between the parties often becomes more and more adversarial and confrontational. The process becomes increasingly tense as each side in effect threatens the other with what the consequences will be if agreement is not reached. As we've seen, unions generally hold the stick of going out on strike or otherwise disrupting the orderly operation of the employer's enterprise. Employers have the potential leverage of locking out the workforce, that is, refusing to allow the workers to report to work as a way putting the squeeze on. Employers also can opt for imposing regressive terms and conditions of employment (that is, making things worse than what the expiring contract provides).

**A Different
Bargaining Style**

"**Interest-based bargaining**" (also known as "**win-win**"), on the other hand, starts from some very different assumptions. This style of negotiation is based on the belief that the parties to a collective bargaining relationship have a joint interest in sharing information and in working together cooperatively to come up with mutually satisfactory resolutions to the issues that they both have a stake in. Because of the cooperation that underlies interest-based bargaining, negotiations that conclude successfully using this model often lead to a less confrontational and more productive relationship between the employer and the union long after the contract is signed.

In interest-based bargaining, all items on the bargaining table, from wages and fringe benefits to how work is to be done, are seen as problems to be solved collegially and creatively by the parties. The style by which this bargaining is conducted reflects these assumptions. For example, rather than having each bargaining team sit directly across from the other at the table, the seating is usually mixed, around a large table. Fewer caucuses are taken, since the bargainers put more effort into brainstorming together to come up with possible solutions to problems than into crafting formal proposals and counterproposals. The communications taking place outside the bargaining room, both to union members and the public at large, are generally far less adversarial and strident in tone than what one generally sees in traditional bargaining. And they are generally more limited in frequency and in scope.

When the union is dealing with an enlightened employer – that is, one genuinely seeking to reach a fair agreement with the union that will serve both parties' interests over time–interest-based bargaining can be an excellent tool. It can enable the union to get information that it might otherwise not have access to, and that information can point the way to new resolutions to stubborn problems. The negotiations process can be a highly efficient one, since the ground rules eliminate the need for most, if not all, posturing by the parties. And particularly in the public sector, where the formal scope of bargaining is usually more restrictive than in the private sector, an interest-based approach to a collective bargaining relationship can be a direct path to a seat at the table with the employer, so that the employees' voice can be heard on a wider range of issues.

But Danger Can Lurk…

But unions sometimes learn the hard way that interest-based bargaining can be filled with danger. Traditional bargaining, whatever its shortcomings, makes it clear which side is for and which side is against any particular proposal to change things in the workplace. The very nature of this style of bargaining means that the union has a great deal of incentive to keep its members aware of what's going on at the bargaining table. A completely uninformed membership is one unlikely to respond when called on to engage in a job action or another show of strength, should that prove necessary.

There are far too many examples in recent years of interest-based bargaining in which unions were not able to maintain sound footing. The mutual-gains approach does require an open atmosphere and sincere efforts toward a cooperative relationship. But unions sometimes overlook the importance of keeping the membership informed about what's happening at the bargaining table and what's at stake in the negotiations. Even as mutual and creative problem solving takes place at the table, the union leadership must take care to educate its members so that they will be committed to taking the necessary action to confront the employer if that proves necessary. Mutual-gains bargaining, of course, doesn't always work. So unions need to do the necessary groundwork so that if settlement is not reached, it will be possible to shift gears on short notice and take on the employer in a real contract fight.

YOUR

union contract

WHAT IT COVERS

If you don't already have one, it's worth getting access to your own copy of the union contract, whether it's online or in print form. Depending on what bargaining law you're covered by, you're probably legally entitled to get a copy from your local union. Don't try to read the collective bargaining agreement cover to cover; unless your social life is very, very empty, it's extremely unlikely that you'll find the entire "union book" gripping reading. But it's worth checking out the table of contents and at least skimming the agreement. You'll probably find that there's much more covered in it than you suspected. You may discover that you have more rights than you realized and the potential for more control over your working life.

What's covered and what's not covered in a collective bargaining agreement varies quite a bit, depending on a lot of factors. Both what legally may be included in the contract and what the contract terms will be on particular subjects are determined by such factors as what bargaining law governs your workplace, the sort of work you do, and what the standard practices are in your industry or geographic area. The discussion below covers items that are typical for union contracts. Keep in mind, though, that every contract is pretty much unique, and that not every workplace rule or agreement is contained in the collective bargaining agreement.

The Essentials: Pay, Benefits and More

Collective bargaining agreements almost always cover the basic dollars-and-cents issues that people think of when they think of a unionized workplace: all aspects of pay, health coverage and other benefits, different types of leave, and the like. But keep in mind one big example of the differences you'll find from one type of contract to another: you may discover that your contract does not cover some of the basic economic aspects of your workplace life because, particularly if you are in the public sector, pay levels and certain benefits like retirement and health care may be decided by law or through another process besides union negotiations at your workplace.

Payday Variations

On items like pay, you may be surprised at the level of detail in the contract. You may find, for example, page after page after page spelling out eligibility for different pay levels, rules for shift or other differentials, when and how you can get a raise, and when – and if – your pay can be cut. The contract may even specify what information is to appear on your pay stub, how frequently you are to be paid, perhaps even when you are entitled to receive your money when the normal payday falls on a holiday, as well as rules concerning direct bank deposit of your pay.

It's common to see different union contracts tackle the same topic in a variety of ways. But the subject of pay determination may be the area in which union contracts display the greatest number of approaches.

Some contracts set forth specific dollar amounts, payable on an hourly or other basis. Under such a setup, all employees performing a particular type of work or all those with certain seniority must be paid at the same rate. Other contracts provide for a base salary, but they also provide for the possibility of "merit pay" or other variables that can vary the pay levels for individual employees.

For some types of work, it's common for the collective bargaining agreement to set only a minimum salary for each classification. Under such a setup, the employer may not pay less than that specified amount but is free to pay anyone more than that. Or, particularly in direct sales jobs and in the food service industry, compensation may consist of a contractually specified base rate plus a formula for commission or provision for tips.

Some contracts set up a "**two-tier pay system**," with newly hired employees coming in at a lower rate and working up a different pay scale. Sometimes, but not always, after a certain number of years these employees catch up in pay to their longer term co-workers. Besides shortchanging these newer workers (who are performing the same work but are not getting equal pay), current employees who vote to approve a contract with such a two-tier system can find themselves outfoxed after some years pass. When they vote in a two-tier system, they think that they've gotten to preserve their own pay levels by having newer hires earn a bit less. But they find that the day comes when the new folks outnumber the old-timers, and that's the day when the new and changed union majority doesn't see any fairness in having the long term employees earn more than they do. Finally, there is also the device of "grandfathering." (Use of the term "grandparenting" has not yet caught on.) "Grandfathered" or "red-circled" employees are those who, despite some change in their job or even the elimination of an entire classification, are entitled under the contract to hold on to their old pay rates (and benefits).

Schedules and Benefits

Your work schedule may well be covered in great detail as well. There may be very specific language dictating who can be involuntarily assigned or who can choose to work on particular days or times, along with pay levels attached to night, weekend or holiday shifts. Supplementing laws already on the books, your contract may define "overtime" and regulate its use/abuse and any extra compensation that comes into play. Depending on the type of work that you do, your contract may guarantee a certain amount of time to get ready to begin work or to wash up at the end of a shift, may define and specify compensation for being on call or for traveling to a particular worksite, or may set mileage reimbursement levels or per diem rates for travel.

There may well be a similar level of detail for benefits. Sometimes an appendix to the contract will include documents that detail what's covered and what's not in the health care plan, life insurance and disability policies, and other benefits.

Many other "essentials" are covered in almost every contract. Here are some that frequently appear.

Holidays and Leave

Your contract probably spells out what holidays are observed. It also will outline the various types of leave – sick and vacation, perhaps parental and bereavement leave, even time off for jury duty – saying how much you're entitled to and under what circumstances, and detailing procedures you may have to follow to use your leave. You may discover that there are types of leave contained in the union contract that are used so seldom you weren't even aware of them. These might include paid or unpaid time off in connection with the birth or adoption of a child, for disability, for a death in the family, or the option of taking unpaid time off or adjusting your work schedule so that you can go back to school.

Job security   Nearly every collective bargaining agreement contains provisions on the discipline of employees. This is not surprising, since there is really no other aspect of employment where the difference between those who are protected by a union contract and those who are not is more dramatic. A fundamental doctrine of American law is known as "**employment at will**." Stripped to its essentials, this means that an employer is within its legal rights if it undertakes disciplinary action, including termination, for no reason – or even for a bad reason. Even if an employer's action is clearly arbitrary, unreasonable, or unfair, "employees at will" have no legal recourse unless there's a specific law forbidding the personnel action. More and more industries in today's economy are taking advantage of this. Companies do this to save costs and to maintain power over their workforce. They even try to market this as a benefit of employment to employees. If you don't have the coverage of a union contract, the only protections you'll have will come from laws or policies that are limited in scope, such as statutes that prohibit certain specified types of discrimination.

But don't be surprised if you see that your contract does not spell out what particular infractions may lead to discipline or what penalty is applied to particular acts of misconduct. Many contracts simply say that there is a "**just cause**" or "**good cause**" standard for dealing out discipline. Don't worry; these words mean a lot more than you might think. They are what are known as legal terms of art, meaning that they have acquired some fairly precise meetings through the history of your workplace, and through thousands of arbitration and court decisions. Rather than attempting to write what would be a pretty thick book, specifying each and every possible infraction, and all the different circumstances that might surround it, most unions and employers simply use "just cause" or "good cause" as a kind of contractual shorthand. Each discipline case is then decided on its own merits, but with the facts at hand being evaluated in light of the detailed standards that have developed over time.

Even if the particular infractions that you can be disciplined for are not specified in the contract, there may well be some specific guidelines that are set out. For example, it is common for a contract to require that "**progressive discipline**" must be followed. This means that ordinarily there must be a series of infractions to justify increasingly severe punishment. So the first time you come in late without notifying your supervisor, you may well receive only an oral or written warning. But if you persist in the same conduct, or engage in other misconduct, the consequences may be far more severe: the penalty can escalate each time, to the point of suspension and eventually termination. Don't get too creative, though, since there are common sense limits to this. You won't get far trying to argue that just because this was only the first time you slugged a co-worker, you can't be terminated on the spot.

A related concept is that "the punishment must fit the crime." Through either general or specific language, the contract will usually make it clear that if there's been only a minor infraction there can be only a minor penalty. So if you're a few minutes late to work a couple of times, the employer couldn't get away with trying to fire you for this.

Your collective bargaining agreement is quite likely to cover the procedures that must be followed if your employer wishes to discipline you. Specifying such procedures is a way of making sure that there is a measure of "**due process**," a concept that covers basic notions of fairness.

For example, your contract may well require that your employer put in writing whatever misconduct or deficiencies in performance it alleges. This serves as the equivalent of a formal complaint or indictment in a court proceeding; it's only fair that you be told what you allegedly have done wrong, so that you can change your behavior or adequately defend yourself. You'll see that your contract probably goes on to provide for some opportunity–either in a meeting or by submitting something in writing–to challenge the allegations against you. Whether spelled out in the contract itself or in a law, your union has the right to be given documents and other information that relate to any charges against you. This may even cover information relating to your co-workers. If, for example, part of your defense is that you are being singled out for harsher punishment than that given out to other employees ("**disparate treatment**"), your union will be able to obtain the records of all others who may have committed similar infractions.

And should your employer not back off, the resulting disciplinary action can be reviewed through the formal grievance/arbitration procedure, covered in Chapters 7 and 8.

Who is Covered Your union contract will not cover everyone in your workplace. Probably on the first page or so, you'll find the definition of the bargaining unit and jurisdiction covered. Whether the boundaries of contract coverage are based on type of work performed, location, or other factors, the agreement itself will set forth who's covered and who's not. And with constant emerging technology and other factors transforming American workplaces at a rapid pace, your contract may even specify how it is to be determined whether new jobs or new types of work that come into existence will or won't be covered by the terms of the contract.

Membership and Dues Your contract will specify what requirements there may be, and what procedures must be followed, for joining or quitting the union, or for paying dues or fees to the union. Most workplaces nowadays provide for dues checkoff – that is, a procedure for having your dues deducted directly from your pay. Your contract will include the procedures that apply to this process as well.

Probationary Period Your contract is likely to specify what "**probationary period**" applies when new employees are hired. During a probationary period an employer is permitted to terminate an employee with little or no justification. Probationary periods can run from as little as thirty days for some less skilled work to a full seven years for college professors.

Job Reductions The contract will also set the criteria under which your employer can cut hours or lay off employees. For example, it may be necessary for the employer to prove that there is a "compelling business necessity" or a "financial emergency" to justify any shrinking of the workforce. And the contract will cover how it is determined which employees get to keep their jobs and which don't. This is often determined by seniority, that is, length of service with the employer. There may be detailed procedures, including such items as how much notice must be given, determination of severance pay, retraining rights, and priority for being rehired in the future.

Do I Pay Dues During My Probationary Period?

Well, it depends. Unions have different practices, based on both policy and practical considerations.

• If the union contract fully covers probationary employees (except for full job security during the probationary period) many unions find it fair to have probationary employees pay dues. After all, those employees are getting the benefits of union-won pay rates, sick leave and vacation time, and so on.

• Some contracts, though, carve out new employees from a great many or most protections and benefits. When this is the case, those employees usually aren't required to pay the full union dues until they get the full contract protections.

• The length of a probationary period also can be a factor in setting a policy on union dues. If the probationary period is 30 or 60 days, it's no big deal if the new employees don't start out paying union dues. But during the 7 years that it takes for professors to get the job security protections that tenure provides, it's reasonable for them to pay the union for all the protections and benefits that they're getting from their first day on the job.

Retirement Options

In addition to whatever regular pension plan or alternative tax-deferred plan is in place, the contract may provide for other options. For example, you may find that once you reach a certain age, or have been with the employer long enough, you may have the right to have a "phased retirement," meaning that you can choose to have a reduced work schedule for a set period of time. Or the contract may allow "buyouts," permitting certain employees to leave with either a cash settlement or a retirement payout.

Health and Safety

Adding to legal protections that are on the books for all employees, your collective bargaining agreement may contain rights for your workplace. Some contracts contain only a general statement that health and safety standards will be respected. Such provisions are more valuable than it may at first appear. This is because such contract language gives the union the right to challenge lax health and safety standards through the grievance/arbitration procedure, rather than having to go outside to a separate agency or to court to try to enforce the law.

Joint Committees

Contracts often set up "**joint labor-management committees**." These are sometimes given specific responsibilities, like monitoring health and safety conditions in the workplace or changes in healthcare benefits. But some joint committees are given full authority to address any matters of concern, whether or not these items are covered elsewhere in the contract or even are negotiable under the technical requirements of the law.

Union Institutional Rights

Most contracts contain language providing resources and tools the union needs to conduct its day-to-day operations: time off needed by stewards to represent members or by negotiators to bargain a new contract, access to the worksite by union representatives, use of the employer's email system or bulletin boards for union notices, and similar guarantees.

Personnel Records

In addition to (or buried deep within) the contract language covering discipline, you may find that you have the right as an individual to review whatever documents have been placed in your personnel file and to submit rebuttal statements to be included in your file.

Duration

Right on the first page or near the very end of the contract you'll find the "**duration clause**." This tells you how long the contract will remain in effect. This is usually measured in years, and it's often three years or more. Sometimes the contract itself spells out under what circumstances its terms will automatically be extended after it expires. You may also find language setting forth the time frames or procedures the parties already have agreed to for bargaining the next contract.

And Even More

You'll find many other topics covered in the contract. It may provide for substance abuse or other counseling services. It may tell you when and where you are allowed to smoke. It may include a policy or rights on social media. It may set standards for personal appearance in the workplace, or rules that apply to wearing name badges or identifying yourself by name to customers, co-workers or the public.

This book can't tell you exactly which provisions are in your contract; but it can guarantee that if you read your union contract you'll find things you never knew were there!

"It's Not in Here!"

Suppose you actually read through your entire union contract, and don't find a particular topic covered that is of interest to you. What might the explanation be, and what can you do about it?

It's possible that the item you're interested in has in fact been addressed by the union and the employer but in a document elsewhere. There may be language on the subject in an employee handbook or other company policy, or in a regulation or statute. Or it may be found in a written memorandum of understanding or other agreement reached by your union and employer, but one that was not included in the printed contract booklet.

And the concept of a longstanding "**past practice**" may create enforceable rights that an arbitrator will read into a collective bargaining agreement, even if there is no specific language in the contract that spells out those practices.

So the first thing you should do is simply ask your union steward for information. You may learn that items of importance to you are *not* covered by the contract or by another written agreement enforceable by the union. There may be a variety of explanations if this is the case: some topics simply as a matter of law may not be included in the contract; or your union may have tried in earlier rounds of bargaining to win certain contract language, but without success; or it may be that particular items never made it to the proposal stage in bargaining, because the bargaining committee and union leadership just weren't aware that those topics were of concern to members, or because they didn't set as high a priority on them as they should have.

No matter what the reason for a topic not being covered by the contract, communication is the order of the day. Asking why something is not included may give you the explanation you need as to where else to look, or why the item can't be addressed in negotiations.

Even if nothing can be done to address your concern at the moment, your inquiry may be a valuable source of input to your union, which needs to know how the contract bargaining process can be put to better use in the future to serve the interests of the members.

Remember: The Union Contract Is a Living Document

Generally, when the parties sign off on a new collective bargaining agreement, they are agreeing to be bound by its terms until a new agreement takes its place some years later. But it's still worth asking your steward about changes you might like to see before then, since there are a couple of exceptions to this general rule.

First, your contract may provide for the kind of joint labor-management committee mentioned above. If this is the case, your union may be able to use such a committee to address your concern. Or sometimes collective bargaining agreements themselves will provide that some of their terms will be up for renegotiation during the life of the contract. The most typical instance is pay during the later years of a contract, but sometimes other events – such as the introduction of new technology – trigger contract provisions that give your union the right to what's called midterm bargaining.

In addition, even if the contract itself doesn't specifically spell this out, quite often the union has the right to bargain over changes that the employer wants to make during the life of a contract. For example, it may be that your employer cannot decide to relocate or to reduce the workforce without first giving the union the opportunity to bargain.

82

grievances:

ENFORCING WORKPLACE LAW

Virtually every union contract contains a grievance/arbitration procedure, which is the way the union and the employer tackle disagreements about workplace rights and obligations covered by the contract. Filing a "**grievance**" is the equivalent of starting a lawsuit: you put in writing what you believe another party has done that is contrary to the law, and what action will be necessary to correct the situation. If after going through a series of procedural steps the dispute is not resolved, then it can go to the last step: "**arbitration**." An arbitration hearing is the equivalent of appearing before a judge in court, where the parties argue the case out and obtain a final ruling, one way or the other, from the neutral arbitrator.

83

What Grievances Can Cover

A grievance is not a device for curing whatever ails you; your contract itself will have a definition of what is and is not covered by the grievance procedure. The most favorable definition of the scope of a grievance, though not the most common one, gives you the right to use the contract grievance procedure to challenge any area of concern connected to your workplace life. More commonly, a grievance will be defined in a more narrow fashion, covering only challenges to specific provisions in the contract.

Quite often, the contract will specify that not all of its terms are subject to challenge through the grievance procedure. Sometimes as a matter of either law or policy, you will be required to seek relief somewhere else. For example, take the case of a member who has a problem with how a health insurance provider has handled a claim. In most cases, there will be a complaint procedure outside of the contract that is designed to deal with that problem and that the member will be required to use. Or it may be that even though your collective bargaining agreement contains language prohibiting certain types of personnel actions, the contract itself may require going to a government agency to enforce those rights.

There can be another type of exclusion from what is covered by the grievance procedure. Because of the way a bargaining law is written or simply as a matter of power at the bargaining table, your employer may have been able to exclude certain matters from being grieved at all. These are often areas of what are termed "**management rights**," that is, matters considered to be enough within the prerogative of the employer that they may simply not be challenged under the union contract's grievance procedure.

Finally, you may find that while some categories of disputes under the contract may be processed through the steps of the grievance procedure, they cannot be taken all the way to arbitration.

A Note of Caution: Insubordination

You may find yourself being told by your supervisor to do something that he or she has no right to insist on under the union contract. The natural temptation is to say, "I know my rights, I'm not doing it!"

But be forewarned about the "**work, then grieve**" rule. This generally accepted notion in the world of labor relations is that you do not have the right to disobey an employer directive, even if that directive is in violation of the collective bargaining agreement. The required response is to do what the employer says, under protest, and then to pursue relief through the grievance procedure. While there are exceptions – such as for dangerous health and safety violations – think twice before risking discipline for insubordination.

Who Can File a Grievance?

Individual members of the bargaining unit – that is, you and your co-workers – usually can initiate grievances yourselves under the contract if you believe that the terms of the collective bargaining agreement have been violated. In fact, the law covering your type of workplace may even provide that you have the right to initiate a grievance with your employer without a union representative even being present. But keep a few things in mind if you consider this course of action. First, the union usually is given the opportunity to be present at any "adjustment" (that is, a settlement) of a grievance. Second, as we will see when we discuss arbitration, it's almost always the case that past a certain level, it is your union, not you as an individual that has the right to elevate the case. And perhaps most important, for your own protection and for the good of your co-workers, it's almost always a good idea to involve your union representative right from the very beginning of pursuing a grievance.

Unions themselves also initiate grievances. As the exclusive representative of everyone in the bargaining unit, the union has the right – and, quite often, also the legal obligation – to use the collective bargaining agreement to challenge the employer's improper or unfair actions. The union will sometimes file grievances over employer conduct that affects everyone in the bargaining unit, for example, if a unilateral employer directive limits everyone's ability to take leave days. The union may also file grievances on behalf of one particular group of employees, such as workers on one shift who are denied proper pay. A third possibility is that sometimes the union itself finds it necessary or politically desirable to initiate a grievance on behalf of a single individual. This may be a useful way to provide some "protection" to that individual, or perhaps to send a message to the employer that the union stands firmly behind this one employee. Finally, if the rights of the union itself have been violated – for example, by not allowing a steward time to meet with a member, if that's a right under the contract – then the union can file a grievance on its own behalf. Although this is not always the case, it may be that your employer also has the right to file grievances under the contract. Since the collective bargaining agreement is a set of rules that both parties are required to live by, it does make sense that either can challenge what it believes are violations of the rules.

Why Grieve?

The natural inclination is to think about pursuing a grievance only if it looks like it has a strong chance of coming up a winner. But what if a union thinks that a case is not going to be a winner if it's taken all the way to arbitration? Does that mean that there's no sense in even filing the grievance in the first place?

Actually, there may be lots of good reasons for a union to file a grievance that it doesn't expect to "win."

Fire a Warning Shot

There are times when it doesn't make sense to think about a fight to the death with the employer on a particular action. It may just not be worth it to arbitrate a relatively minor erosion of existing working conditions, or what looks like a one-time event that's not likely to come up again. At the same time, rather than do nothing, a group grievance could serve to put the employer on notice that its action has not gone unnoticed, and that if it does try the same maneuver again, it may well have a serious fight on its hands.

Shine A Light

One of the most frustrating experiences in the life of a union representative is to hear an employer say, "That's just you complaining; none of the people you say you represent even care." Sometimes it takes a formal grievance filed by an employee – or two or three or more – to get the employer to acknowledge that a particular problem is real and needs to be addressed.

Build a Record

One not entirely humorous definition of paranoia is "a heightened appreciation of reality." Sometimes it's hard to know where to draw a line between an isolated memo taking you to task for something and the first deadly serious shot in your supervisor's war against you. So even if all you know is that there *may* be a suspension or termination action looming in your future, sometimes the wisest course of action is to begin to build a written record in your defense now.

Forge Employee Unity

It may be that for one reason or another an immediate practical resolution of a particular problem may not be in the cards. But a grievance (particularly a group grievance) might be just what is needed to start building solidarity among those wronged by a particular supervisor or policy. If you and others can get it together enough to take a small action, like filing a grievance, this may be the first step toward you and your co-workers later doing whatever it takes to fight – and win – on this or a bigger issue.

An Overview of the Grievance Procedure

All grievance procedures require going through a series of steps. The contract itself identifies when each step is to take place, what precisely is to occur, and who may or must be involved at each stage of the process. Generally, the procedures get more formal as you go through each of the steps. Some grievances are resolved successfully at the earlier stages of the process, while others are not pursued past a certain point for a variety of reasons. Before we take a look at what the steps of the grievance procedure look like, here are a few notes of caution.

First, if you read through the grievance procedures contained in your collective bargaining agreement, some of it may look like fairly technical stuff. You'll probably find requirements as to the format that must be followed in writing up grievances, the rules for who receives certain grievance filings, calculation of time frames for processing a grievance (such as the difference between "working days" and "calendar days"), and the like.

Don't be intimidated by any of this, because your union steward has received training in how to process grievances and has additional help to call on if needed. The best advice for you is, don't try to wing it! As soon as something happens that you think might properly be challenged through the grievance procedure, consult with your steward.

Second, you are to be commended if you familiarize yourself with the provisions of your contract. But a word of caution: maybe the plain language of the contract makes it sound like you can't file a grievance, but sometimes even seemingly clear contractual language doesn't mean what it says and you may still have grounds for a grievance. For example, maybe it's clear that too many days have gone by since a particular event occurred for you to meet the time frame set forth in the contract for initiating a grievance. But it's worth at least consulting with your steward, since you may learn that there are sometimes unwritten exceptions even to such seemingly clear-cut provisions, such as the time clock stopping for holidays. Or you may learn that there are other mechanisms besides the grievance procedure that can be used to address the problem.

And third, don't make the mistake of assuming that it would be useless to pursue a grievance because you think you'd never be able to get enough evidence to prove your case. The fact is, your union has the legal right to obtain vast quantities of documents and other information from your employer if that information is needed to evaluate a potential or pending grievance. If proof of your grievance over unfair treatment lies in determining how your employer has dealt with co-workers under circumstances similar to yours, your union will be able to get hold of the relevant personnel records.

The Steps of a Grievance

Before just about any workplace complaint is put into writing, an attempt should be made to work through the problem at the lowest level. Even if your contract's grievance procedure doesn't specifically call for an informal, oral step to start out with, you and/or your union steward should talk to a supervisor in an attempt to clear up any misunderstandings or to resolve any disagreement. This is almost always a good idea, in part because once a complaint is committed to writing, parties' positions tend to harden. And even if an informal attempt to address a problem does not in fact resolve it, it generally has the beneficial effect of at least clarifying what the problem is and how the parties may see it differently.

If informal attempts don't work, the next step consists of formally putting the grievance in writing. The contract may require a certain amount of detail in this process, such as identifying the specific contract provisions that you allege have been violated. But generally the idea is simply to lay out, at least in general terms, that an identified action taken by the employer is being challenged, and that certain relief is sought. Your contract itself may contain a sample form to be used to initiate a grievance.

One or more face-to-face meetings take place following the filing of a formal written grievance. At each stage, the participants on each side generally will be higher up in each organization's food chain. At these meetings, the union and employer representatives try to hash out whether they agree on what the facts are, whether the contract has in fact been violated, and if so, what it will take to resolve the grievance. The employer usually is required to furnish the union with a written response after each meeting, setting forth its position. If the union chooses to kick the grievance up to the next step, it likewise generally is required to do this in writing.

Your Role in the Process

What is your role in processing a grievance through the steps? First, of course, it is your job initially to approach your union representative and report the problem as you see it. You will need to set forth the facts as accurately as you can and to make sure that your representative understands not only what has happened, but why it is a matter of concern to you and, perhaps, your co-workers as well. As the grievance case goes on, your steward or union grievance committee may well need additional information to evaluate or to process the grievance. Since you have a stake in the outcome, you should be prepared to assist them in obtaining any needed information.

A number of factors having to do with the specific procedures in your contract and with the labor relations process in general will dictate whether it is advisable or even possible for both you and a union representative to attend grievance meetings. In some instances, you may be tempted to go it alone and argue your case yourself. But keep in mind that when it comes to labor relations matters such as processing a grievance, your union representative has been trained to do the job. So usually what makes the most sense at a grievance meeting is for you to play a support role and let your union representative take the lead in presenting and arguing the grievance.

There may be reasons for it to be the wisest course of action for you not to be present at all at a particular meeting, such as the danger of an unhelpful personality clash between you and a supervisor. But generally, you can and should play a positive role by attending a grievance meeting. Factual matters may come up during the meeting that you are in the best position to evaluate and to respond to. And besides, this is your "day in court," so it makes sense for you to be able to observe firsthand what is being said.

At the grievance meeting itself, you should be more than a passive onlooker, since your first hand knowledge can be very valuable. In order to contribute effectively, both you and your union representatives should be setting aside whatever time is needed before and after meetings with the employer to go over the case and to discuss and plan the next steps.

Relief Available Under the Grievance Procedure

An important consideration in deciding whether and how to pursue any grievance is the question of what you can get if you win, often called "**relief**." Though the language of your contract's grievance procedure will determine in large part what can be obtained by filing a grievance, it's useful to understand that there are certain general categories of remedies.

Perhaps the most clear-cut type of relief that can be obtained through the grievance procedure is in those cases where one or more individuals have suffered a direct and measurable financial harm. For example, if a two-week suspension is overturned, a "**make whole remedy**" will include payment of lost wages and restoration of any benefits, such as payment into a retirement plan, or accrual of leave. There may also be nonfinancial consequences that can be remedied through the grievance procedure, such as cleaning up the employee's personnel file by deleting references to the suspension.

In grievances that challenge an employer action, such as the improper issuance of a new workplace policy, a successful resolution would include withdrawing that policy. If your employer takes an action that is in violation of a provision of the contract, appropriate relief might include an agreement that similar employer actions will not take place in the future.

For all sorts of reasons, it is in both parties' interests for an employer and a union to work together successfully to resolve a pending grievance. For one thing, creative solutions can often be devised by those most familiar with the situation, and this can pave the way for everyone ending up satisfied with the outcome. By contrast, when a case goes all the way to an outside arbitrator for a hearing and a final decision, the types of relief that are possible are usually fairly restricted. It is not uncommon for the contract itself to set certain limits on what the arbitrator has the power to order, such as limiting the arbitrator's ability to reduce the penalty in a disciplinary action.

And even if your union contract itself does not contain restrictions on what constitutes appropriate relief, there are commonly accepted limitations on the authority of arbitrators. For example, arbitrators cannot award "punitive damages" or damages for "pain and suffering," which you might be able to get in civil litigation. But before you start thinking, "To heck with the grievance procedure, I'll just go to court," be forewarned that quite often the law says that an aggrieved party is required to go through the grievance process rather than just filing a lawsuit.

Finally, any time the final resolution of a dispute is placed in the hands of a third party, there is the risk of ending up with a decision that just "splits the difference." Often this is done awkwardly enough that neither side to the dispute walks away satisfied.

Creative unionists keep in mind the importance of not only the content of a grievance but how a grievance is filed and pursued. With a bit of thought about the
underlying dynamics in a workplace, the union can use the filing of a grievance
as a tactical tool, to educate and mobilize members, or to send a message to the
employer.

Let's consider first the format used to file a grievance. Suppose that an employer
has denied requests for approved leave submitted by a number of employees. The
union believes that this violates a provision in the contract, and it decides to challenge the employer. One possibility – the most obvious one – is for the union
itself to file a single grievance on behalf of all those affected by the employer's
action. Procedurally, this results in the employer having to respond one time, to
one grievance, as it deals with the union as the party pursuing the grievance.

But there are other possible ways to pursue such a matter. The union might
choose, for example, to initiate a "**group grievance**," with individual employees each signing on to the initial written grievance. Attacking the problem this
way can have the advantage of promoting a sense of participation on the part of
each individual who actually puts pen in hand and signs. And getting individual
signatures from each employee affected means that the union has to reach out
and explain to each employee why the employer's action violates the collective
bargaining agreement, and that the union is doing something about it. Finally,
consider the difference in these two methods of pursuing this grievance from
the point of view of the employer. A grievance signed individually by a number
of employees is like a petition; it sends a clear message to the employer that its
response will be observed and evaluated not just by the union as an organization
but by real-life members, too.

Now consider yet a third possible way to pursue such a grievance: a mass filing
of grievances. A very effective tactic to put pressure on an employer can be for the
union to organize a large number of employees to each file an individual grievance on a particular matter. This results in a much bigger expenditure of time
and effort on the employer's part, as it is forced to individually process numerous
grievances. And it may send the clearest message of all that there is a problem to
be dealt with, and that that problem has been identified as such by a great many
individuals, not "just the union."

And there are creative ways to process a grievance through the procedural steps so as to involve and educate members as well as put pressure on the employer. For example, many contracts contain provisions authorizing a grievant to be released from normal work duties to prepare for or to participate in grievance meetings with the employer. So if the union has chosen to file a large number of individual grievances, rather than one grievance covering all the affected individuals, the employer will have to contend with releasing quite a few people from their normal work assignments.

Or at an even earlier stage, your contract may provide that you are to meet with your immediate supervisor to discuss a potential grievance even before the grievance is reduced to writing. In this instance, there can be immediate pressure brought to bear on the employer if a large number of individuals chooses the same moment to stop doing their regular work because they need to talk to their supervisors – right now! – about a potential grievance.

Direct Action: Better Than a Grievance?

There's no question that the ability to use the grievance/arbitration procedure to challenge employer violations of the terms of the collective bargaining agreement is one of the most potent weapons in the union arsenal. Every day, American unions successfully use contractual grievance procedures to win back the jobs of fired members, to protect wages and benefits, to prevent employers from closing down entire workplaces, and much else. Obtaining relief through pursuing a grievance, perhaps all the way to arbitration, is less costly, less risky, and less disruptive than if the union had to go to court or lead its members out on a strike.

But as effective and efficient as grievance procedures can be, the advantages are often accompanied by a number of disadvantages: the long time it often takes to resolve the dispute, the cost in union dollars and time to fight cases, and the shifting of direct control over the problem and its resolution from the affected employees to union officials, staffers, and attorneys.

Because of the drawbacks that can accompany the use of a grievance procedure, sometimes employees and their unions are better off if they can take direct action to force a wayward employer to mend its ways. Especially with a cynical employer, one who may count on the passage of time or the limited relief available through a grievance procedure working in its favor, what's needed is a direct, quick, "in your face" demonstration of the employees' will.

Take, for example, the all too common situation of an employer determined to remove work being done by unionized employees from the protections of the union contract. In one case, a company sought to lay off its unionized cafeteria workers and contract out the work to a nonunion company. The union might well have had a strong grievance challenging the employer's move to throw its members out on the street, and six months or a year later might well have gotten an arbitrator to rule in its favor. But the unionized employees in the building came up with a much quicker and more dramatic way to demonstrate to the employer that its planned actions would have serious consequences: everyone (except for managers, of course) stopped buying food in the cafeteria. The message to the employer was clear and immediate: unless you reach an acceptable accommodation with us as to who's going to work in this cafeteria, this cafeteria isn't going to do much business! The employer got the message, and all of the cafeteria workers stayed on the company payroll.

94

BREAK GLASS

arbitration:

THE END OF THE LINE

When a grievance does not get resolved by the last step of the grievance procedure, you find yourself at the end of the line: arbitration. While each of the meetings that take place at the various steps of the grievance procedure is sort of a mini-"day in court," an arbitration hearing is pretty much the real thing. An arbitrator is a neutral third party, usually an attorney, selected jointly by the employer and the union. Professional arbitrators function much as judges do in regular courts of law. Arbitrators swear in witnesses, rule on who can testify and on what evidence can be introduced. The payment for the arbitrator's services and certain costs associated with the process are usually split fifty-fifty by the employer and the union.

A private organization, the American Arbitration Association, and a federal agency, the Federal Mediation and Conciliation Service, are two organizations that provide lists of qualified arbitrators to unions and employers in both the private and public sectors. In addition, many states have their own lists of arbitrators for use by public employers and unions. Usually a new arbitrator is selected to hear each arbitration case, but sometimes the parties to a collective bargaining relationship will use a set group of "permanent arbitrators" or "umpires," to hear all arbitration cases. And sometimes an arbitration board hears a case, with one neutral arbitrator joined by two others: one appointed by the union, the other by the employer.

Almost always, the arbitrator has the authority to make a final decision that is binding on both parties. This makes the right to go to arbitration an extremely powerful weapon in the union's arsenal. Unlike the steps of the grievance procedure, in which a series of close-minded employer representatives can just keep saying, "speak to the hand 'cause the face ain't listening," the employer knows that at the end of an arbitration proceeding, there will be a final, enforceable determination.

But be aware that in some instances, spelled out in the union contract, only advisory arbitration takes place. This means that the arbitrator has the power only to issue a recommendation that the parties are free to accept or reject. Since an award of this type does not have the force of law, enforcement rests with whatever forces of persuasion and agitation the union and its members can bring to bear. In such situations, unions often can in fact create enough pressure to get what they want. The arbitrator's ruling, even if it's not legally binding, gives the union the high moral ground in that fight.

In some ways, an arbitration proceeding is an even more powerful tool for the union than a courtroom trial would be. For one thing, resolving a dispute through arbitration is almost always quicker, easier, and less expensive than taking a case to court. For another, unlike a judge's decision, there are usually fewer opportunities for an employer unhappy with the ruling of an arbitrator to challenge that ruling or to have it overturned on appeal. And consequently, there are fewer opportunities available for an employer who believes that "justice delayed is justice denied, and that's a good thing" deliberately to delay the final resolution of a dispute.

What to Expect If Your Grievance Is Going to Hearing

If your case goes all the way to arbitration, you can expect that some time, usually months, will pass between the employer's final rejection of the grievance and the actual arbitration hearing. Some of this delay is unavoidable, since often the employer and the union will have to go through an agreed upon process to select an arbitrator and to set a hearing date that will fit everyone's schedule.

But participants in the process can put that time to good use for preparation. Just as with processing a grievance through the steps of the grievance procedure, there may well be the need for intensive investigation of the facts to get ready for the hearing. You may need to locate witnesses to any disputed events or to track down the history of other occurrences that may factor into your case. And you, or others who may be called to testify at the arbitration hearing, will need to prepare to give testimony.

The representatives of both sides and the arbitrator will have work to do in advance of the hearing. Your representative, for example, may be trying to get documents or other evidence from the other side to help build your case. And the arbitrator may be pushing both sides to define the issues to be presented to the arbitrator for resolution and to determine what witnesses will be testifying and which documents may be admitted as evidence.

The Arbitration Process

If you've got a basic idea of what takes place in a courtroom trial, you've already got a fairly good notion of what to expect at an arbitration hearing. The major difference is that arbitrations are conducted in a less formal way than court proceedings. For example, you'll never see an arbitrator wearing a judge's robe.

Be prepared for the remote possibility that your union would prefer not to have you present at the hearing, for a variety of reasons. The union may make a tactical decision, for example, that your case will be a stronger one if you aren't subject to cross examination by the employer. In that situation, it might be better for you to not be present, since if you are the other side might be able to force you to testify as their witness. Although it is unlikely that your union may want you to not attend the hearing, it can happen. So take it upon yourself to work out well in advance of the hearing whether you will be present. Since it is your "day in court," you should agree not to attend only if you are satisfied that the union has a legitimate reason to make such a request.

Assuming that you will be present, here's an overall view of what you can expect on the day of the arbitration hearing.

The Hearing   The hearing itself will take place in a regular meeting room of some sort, with the arbitrator sitting either at a separate table up front or at the head of a large conference table. Those on the union side – you, perhaps one or more stewards or grievance officials – will sit together. You'll be sitting next to the union's advocate at the arbitration, who often is a labor lawyer, but sometimes is a union official or staff member who's been trained in how to present a case at arbitration. Another table will consist of a similarly composed group from the employer's side. There may also be an official court reporter producing a transcript of the proceedings for the use of both parties and the arbitrator.

After some preliminary matters, such as determining what issues will be decided by the arbitrator and what witnesses and evidence will be presented, the formal hearing will begin. Depending on the type of case, either the union or the employer will go first in presenting its case, beginning with an opening statement in which the representative outlines what the case is all about. Usually, witnesses testify under oath, first on direct examination (that is, they answer questions asked by the representative of the party calling the witness) and then on cross examination. The arbitrator, too, may choose to ask questions.

Periodically the arbitrator may need to resolve some procedural or other matter, or for another reason may go "**off the record**." This means that the court reporter will take a break and there will be no official transcript of this part of the hearing. Sometimes the arbitrator will talk directly and privately with only the parties' representatives.

When all the evidence is in, sometimes the representatives offer closing arguments to the arbitrator. The arbitrator may issue a "**bench decision**," meaning that the ruling in the case will be made then and there. But more often, the parties will submit written post-hearing briefs, and the arbitrator's award will come down in written form some time after the close of the hearing.

Which Cases Go to Arbitration, and Which Don't

By necessity, unions are forced to be quite selective about which cases get processed all the way to arbitration. Depending on the size of the workplace, dozens or hundreds of grievances may be filed each year. Cases that go all the way to arbitration are quite time consuming and labor intensive and can cost the union treasury many thousands of dollars.

Your Role in Arbitration

At all stages of the grievance/arbitration process, your role is to assist your union representatives in pursuing and processing the case. It's not enough simply to file a grievance and then figure that the union will do the necessary work to win it. As a very practical matter, you are likely to be familiar with facts that your union representatives are not, so you need to stay involved at all stages so that you can provide important input. You also owe it to yourself and to the union to be involved every step of the way, so that you can have a realistic outlook if the question of settlement comes up at any stage of the processing of the case.

At the arbitration hearing itself, the human dynamics can get a little tricky. The last thing you want is for the other side or the arbitrator to get the impression that you and the union representatives are not completely in sync. So make sure that you understand pretty clearly what is going to take place at the hearing before you enter the room. Work this out with your representative, but usually it will be preferable for you to write notes during the hearing itself, rather than try to talk to your representative, which is likely to be too distracting. There will be plenty of breaks during the day during which you can talk things over.

Keep in mind that it is natural for it to take a fair amount of time to complete the arbitration process. And even after the "**final and binding**" arbitration award is issued, either party to a case may pursue an appeal in court. The grounds for overturning an arbitration award are very narrow, though. So unions file appeals very seldom. And nine times out of ten when an employer files an appeal, this is just one more item in their bag of tricks to delay and add unnecessary expense to the union's pursuit of justice.

So while you have every right to be insistent about being informed about the progress of your case, you also have an obligation to be reasonable in your expectations about how quickly it will be resolved.

In deciding which cases can be taken to arbitration, unions must take into account quite a few factors. Obviously, one prime consideration in choosing whether a particular case can justify the time and expense involved in going to arbitration is how likely it is that the case will come up a winner. It stands to reason that grievances that are slam-dunk winners are far more likely to be taken to arbitration than long shot cases.

But here, as with everything else in life, all things are not equal. So here are just some of the questions your union must ask in deciding the best way to allocate its limited resources in the grievance/arbitration process.

How Many are Affected?

The outcome of an individual grievance, by definition, directly affects only one person. But a group grievance, or a grievance filed on behalf of the entire bargaining unit, stands to yield a lot more "bang for the buck" if it is successfully pursued to arbitration.

What Is Its Value as a Precedent?

Some grievances may be important for a particular individual, but they arise out of unusual occurrences or seldom used provisions of the contract. It is considerably more tempting for a union to go all the way to arbitration in a case where the outcome will likely affect others in the future, such as the first "test case" grievance that arises under important language just negotiated into a contract.

Is There Alternative Relief Available?

In some situations it may be that an equally effective alternative to a grievance exists. The union may be able to go to a government agency that has enforcement authority or to use political channels to bring pressure to bear, or you and your co-workers may be able to apply some direct pressure on the employer to successfully address the issue.

What Is the Severity of the Problem?

Terminations (the "capital punishment of the workplace") understandably will be higher on your union's list of priorities than, say, a warning letter that is placed in an employee's personnel file.

Is This the Right Case to Address the Issue?

Your grievance may address a legitimate problem, but another grievance might be a better test case, because it has clearer facts or because the company representative involved handled it less intelligently. So it might make the most sense for the union to take a pass on your case but to go for a victory using another employee's grievance.

What Is the Organizing Potential?

Sometimes pursuing a particular grievance or going all the way to arbitration is part of a larger strategy on the part of the union to address a problem. Perhaps, the publicity surrounding an arbitration case is just one component of the union's plan to raise awareness about a dispute with the employer among those in the workplace or in the community, or to mobilize support for a particular fight.

Keeping the Employer Honest

As you can see, an arbitration proceeding can be quite a time consuming procedure and it can eat up large chunks of the union treasury. So all things being equal, it's almost always better if problems can be tackled and resolved right when they arise: the results are quicker, less costly, and you and your co-workers get to enjoy whatever benefits result more quickly.

But it will always be necessary to take at least some grievance cases to arbitration. Sometimes the employer just won't give in at the outset. So if a problem is important enough, the union needs to have the resolve and the means to take the case all the way to a final arbitration decision. It's also necessary from time to time to fight a case to the end – and win it – to keep the employer honest the next time a workplace grievance arises.

WHERE DO

workplace rights

COME FROM?

As a union member, your workplace rights come from a number of different sources. Let's take a look at the main kinds of employment protection, so that you can better understand where your rights come from and how you can use your union to protect them.

Society has laws that everyone is supposed to live by, passed by legislatures. Similarly, our workplace has its own book of statutes, the collective bargaining agreement. We've taken a look at how a union contract is created through the bargaining process, which is very different from the process used to create laws. The end result is the same, however: a collection of rules that apply to everyone in the workplace, workers and bosses alike, setting forth some things that can be done, other things that must be done, and still others that are totally prohibited. And when someone believes that the rules have been violated, there is the enforcement mechanism of the grievance/arbitration procedure, as we have seen.

Contracts are of varying lengths. Some have a duration of as little as one year, some can go for ten, but most tend to run for several years or so. No matter how long a contract is in effect, though, it stands as the law of the workplace.

Beyond the Contract

The collective bargaining agreement negotiated by your union is the key document affecting your life at work. But not all of the workplace "rules" are found in the union contract. So it's important to understand what sources besides the written word of the union contract establish workplace rights and responsibilities.

Government Laws and Regulations

Many laws apply specifically to workplaces. These may be passed at the federal, state or local level, and some of them are accompanied by rather lengthy regulations that go into great detail. Some, such as wage and hour laws, health and safety statutes, and laws against discrimination, apply to both unionized and non-unionized workplaces. Others come into play in workplaces where the employees are organizing or already have unionized. The most important of the laws dealing with workplace rights will be discussed later in this chapter.

Employer Handbooks and Regulations

If you work for a company, especially a big one, chances are good that there's a handbook with all sorts of rules on things like attendance, dealing with customers, and lots of other specifics about what's allowed and not allowed on the job. Similarly, the typical government employer has agency regulations that control scheduling of time off, how inclement weather days are determined, and countless other topics. These are areas that may or may not be addressed in the union contract. The specific terms of a contract are usually the last word. But they are not necessarily the only word; they may well be supplemented by rules in documents like handbooks and agency regulations.

Unwritten Laws

Besides what's in the contract, or in the employer's handbook or government regulations, every workplace has its unwritten rules. Just as in everyday life, there are ways of doing things in the workplace that may not be written on a page anywhere to read but are accepted by everyone. When you're waiting to get on an elevator, where is it written that you are required to make way for a parent with a toddler? Nowhere, but people understand that that's the way it should be, so that's the way it usually is. Similarly, it may not be written anywhere that it's okay to knock off a little early if you're working Christmas Eve, or that a phone call to check on your children at home is allowed, but that may have developed into the "law of the shop" in your workplace. The U.S. Supreme Court has recognized what it called "industrial common law" as being part of the set of binding workplace rules.

Depending on what your collective bargaining agreement says, it may be that the way things are in your workplace – called established **past practices** – are actually enforceable under the contract or in another legal forum. Arbitrators resolving contract disputes will sometimes rule that employees have the right to do something the way it's always been done, even if there's no explicit language saying so in the contract. The test is whether the practice is a clear one, consistently followed over a long period of time, and accepted by both parties.

For example, at night you may park in a close-by customer lot because that's where everyone always parks, even though the contract doesn't say anything about parking. Suppose one day your employer puts up a sign prohibiting employee parking in the customer lot. The union may well have a grievance it can win that the "past practice" of parking in that lot can't be changed unilaterally. Here's another example. if the employer always has allowed a "grace period" of five minutes before someone is written up as tardy, the union could file a grievance if a worker is disciplined for being four minutes late one day.

Union Constitutions and Bylaws

Your union will also have a constitution and bylaws. These may exist for your local union, your international union or for an intermediate level, like a county or state union body. Generally these documents outline the structure of the union, and say how the union is governed. They will identify the various officers of the union and their authority as well as lay out different election or appointment mechanisms. Procedures dealing with how union meetings are called and how the meetings are conducted will be detailed, specifying who can vote on ratifying a collective bargaining agreement, for example.

The Basic Labor and Employment Law Framework

Most people are surprised to learn how many laws are on the books that regulate the workplace lives of workers, both union and non-union.

There are laws at the federal, state and local levels that apply only in a union context: laws that govern the right to organize a union, the collective bargaining relationship between an employer and its unionized workforce, and the internal rights and responsibilities of unions and their members. And both you and employees who are not represented by a union are covered by a host of other laws. So in many instances, you as a unionized employee have the best of both worlds: statutory protections provided to all employees, plus the additional protections your union has been able to negotiate in your particular workplace.

Let's take a look at the overall scheme of labor laws, followed by a brief overview of some of the more important laws covering both unionized and non-unionized workplaces.

The Private Sector

The National Labor Relations Act (NLRA) is the law establishing union rights for most, though not all, employees. The NLRA was passed in 1935 as the Wagner Act, and has been amended a number of times since then. Its coverage extends to most employees who do not work for a public employer.

If you are in the private sector, it was probably under Section 7 of the NLRA that your union exercised its legal right to organize. If you are a public sector employee, your union rights probably are very similar to those in the NLRA (we'll discuss those shortly). That Act states: "Employees shall have the right to self-organization, to form, join, or assist labor organizations, to bargain collectively through representatives of their own choosing, and to engage in other concerted activities for the purpose of collective bargaining or other mutual aid or protection, and shall also have the right to refrain from any or all such activities . . ."

The National Labor Relations Board, a large federal agency with regional offices in many states, enforces the terms of the act. More likely than not, it was the NLRB that received the union authorization cards signed by you and your co-workers (or those who preceded you in your workplace) and then conducted the union representation election that resulted in your union acquiring formal collective bargaining rights.

Though it functions on an administrative level, the NLRB has a parallel setup to our system of criminal laws. Either because of the words used in the statute itself, or because of regulations or court decisions, certain actions on the part of an employer or a union are defined as unfair labor practices, or ULPs. These ULPs may arise out of actions that take place in a non-union workplace, in the course of a union organizing drive, or after a union already has representation rights. When an unfair labor practice charge is filed, the NLRB first functions as an investigator, gathering evidence from both sides to see whether there are sufficient grounds to believe that the law was violated. If the NLRB regional director decides that it does appear that the law was breached, then a formal complaint is issued, and an NLRB attorney then serves, in effect, as a prosecutor in the case. A separate branch of the NLRB provides a judge, who conducts a hearing and rules on whether the law was broken.

What are the basic categories of employer conduct that are illegal under the NLRA? Violations of the Section 7 rights include:

- statements or actions that interfere with, restrain, or coerce union activity;

- domination of unions (that is, any form of a "company union," where the employer is actually controlling the union);

- discrimination against employees who engage in union activity;

- retaliation against individuals who file unfair labor practice charges or who cooperate with the NLRB in pursuing such charges;

- refusal to engage in good faith bargaining with the union.

Keep in mind that, through years of case decisions, these basic rights are given a broader scope than the words themselves might indicate. For example, the right to engage in union activity includes various types of "**concerted activity**." Suppose the air conditioning system in your workplace keeps breaking down, and it's a hot July. If you and some co-workers gripe to a supervisor about the discomfort, even independent of a formal grievance under your union contract, any retaliation against you by your employer may well be found to violate your rights under the NLRA. And the protections of labor law keep up with new technologies. So just as griping around the water cooler in the old days had legal protection, so too does the more modern griping that can take place on social media.

For a variety of reasons, the NLRB has become less and less predictable in its interpretation of the law, and less consistent in protecting employee and union rights. There are a few primary reasons for this:

• At any given time, there may be underfunding – often quite deliberate – by Congress. This results in cases taking far too long to get processed, which consumes unions' and employees' limited resources.

• Depending on the politics of Congress and the White House at any given time, on a cyclical basis we see anti-worker and anti-union decisions on the part of ideological conservatives who are appointed to the top positions in the NLRB.

• Similarly, the political party in power has control over appointments to the federal courts. So judges who are anti-union in their thinking can overturn labor board rulings that are protective of union rights.

All in all, the balance between an employer's rights and those of employees and their unions is often tilted in the employer's direction.

As a result of anti-union, anti-employee interpretation and enforcement of the national labor law, unions try to find alternatives to having to use NLRB procedures. For example, to avoid lengthy delays in scheduling and conducting elections, many unions now try to force an employer to recognize the union without going through the process of petitioning the board for a representation election. Or unions may try to pressure an employer to change its behavior through other means, by taking direct action or by bringing political pressure to bear, rather than by filing an unfair labor practice charge or going to the courts. But just the same, at least sometimes the board is an effective enforcer of union rights, and many a terminated union activist has been reinstated with full back pay, plus interest, plus reinstatement of lost benefits, as a result of successfully pursuing an unfair labor practice charge.

Law as a Seesaw

Of course, it's always been the case that legislatures exercise their right to change what "the law" says about different subjects. But increasingly these days, even when the written words of a statute (or the U.S. Constitution, for that matter) don't change, a new labor board or new judges in the court system will rule that what "the law" means is exactly the opposite of what it used to mean.

Take the situation of graduate students who work as teaching or research assistants in order to help cover the costs of their education. There's a legal question as to whether the fact that they are students means that they therefore cannot *also* be "employees," which determines whether or not they are covered under the National Labor Relations Act. For a long period after the NLRA was first passed, graduate student employees *did not* have legal protection if they wanted to unionize. Then, in 2000, the labor board ruled that they *did* have the right to unionize. Then, in 2004, the labor board ruled that they *did not* have the right to unionize. Then, in 2016, the labor board ruled that they *did* have the right to unionize. Then, the business-friendly Republican appointees got back in the majority, and...well, you get the drift...

When this kind of back and forth happens – when workers lose their legal right to union representation – whether they can continue to have union representation no longer depends on what the law says. The union's continued role in the workplace simply becomes a question of how strong the union is. There are countless examples of unions that continued bargaining contracts and filing grievances even after they lost the legal right to do so, simply because the employer knew that it couldn't get away with walking away from that collective bargaining relationship.

Limitations . . . and Other Private Sector Labor Law Coverage

The National Labor Relations Act covers only those industries engaged in "interstate commerce." This means that the company in question must conduct at least some business across state lines, and that it must meet a specified "volume of business" standard. As a practical matter, the vast majority of private employers are subject to the provisions of the Act.

But even if a particular employer is subject to the provisions of the NLRA, that law nevertheless does not include in its coverage certain types of workers. Those who are considered "**supervisors**," "**managers**" or "**confidential employees**" are excluded from the protections of the Act. And those classified as "**independent contractors**," a rapidly growing category in the "gig economy," have to fight to get themselves covered by the protections of this federal law. Many companies now force these workers to sign documents saying that they are "independent contractors," a practice known as "**misclassifying employees**." But the bottom line on a legal challenge is always whether these individuals meet the law's definition of an "employee" with union representation rights, not what some piece of paper says.

As outrageous as it might seem, when Congress first passed the Wagner Act (the law that is now known as the National Labor Relations Act), it decided that two categories of poorly paid and mistreated workers *most* in need of union rights

"To Live Outside the Law You Must be Honest": How Postal Workers Won Their Union

Before 1970, postal workers (like other federal employees at the time) had no legal right to unionize and to bargain. But by the end of the year, they were covered by the protections of the National Labor Relations Act. How did this change come about?

On March 18 of that year some postal workers in New York City, on their own, set up picket lines. Before long, 200,000 postal workers nationwide were part of the largest wildcat strike in U.S. history. (A "**wildcat strike**" is when workers decide to just walk off the job, without having a union officially call a strike.) When they shut down mail service from coast to coast, President Nixon mobilized the National Guard to try and deliver the mail. On the eighth day of the strike, the government cried "uncle." The workers not only got a huge pay raise (14% that year!) but they also won the legally protected right to engage in collective bargaining, under the coverage of the NLRB.

– agricultural laborers and domestic workers – would not be covered by the NLRA or by any other federal labor law granting the right to unionize. At the time, the vast majority of both agricultural workers and domestic workers were people of color and immigrants to the U.S., and the vast majority of domestic workers were female. It wouldn't be unfair to conclude that Congress disenfranchised these two categories of workers precisely because then – as now – they mostly weren't white males.

Nevertheless, there is some good news to offset the bad: undocumented workers in other industries *are* covered by the protections of the NLRA.

Adding to the confusing patchwork of labor laws, progressive states sometimes pass their own legislation covering a group of employees that has been excluded from NLRA coverage. To its credit, in 1944 Hawaii did so for farmworkers in that state, and in 1975 California did the same.

To make things just a bit more confusing, certain groups of employees in the private sector who are not covered by the NLRA do have union rights under another federal statute. The nation's oldest labor law, the **Railway Labor Act (RLA)**, was passed in 1926. As you would guess from its title, this law originally covered those in the railway industry. But times changed, and so did the coverage of this statute. Now, the Railway Labor Act governs most work in the airline industry, as well as employees of FedEx, but not UPS (don't give yourself a headache trying to figure that one out). If this law covers you, be aware that it establishes rules for labor-management relations that differ, sometimes significantly, from those in the NLRA. For example, to win union representation rights, the RLA requires a majority of all workers, not just a majority of those actually voting, to cast a ballot for the union. This means that workers who don't participate in the election are counted as "no" votes.

The Public Sector

The protections of the National Labor Relations Act do not extend to regular public sector employees. And a handful of states (particularly in the union-unfriendly South) actually go so far as to outlaw collective bargaining for some or all of their public employees. Overall, only a minority of public sector workers nationwide have union rights. A majority of the states, however, grant at least many public sector workers a statutorily covered right to organize and to engage in collective bargaining.

Federal Employees

Thanks to an executive order issued by President Kennedy in 1962, most federal employees gained the right to unionize. In 1978, Congress solidified this by enacting the **Civil Service Reform Act (CSRA.)** The **Federal Labor Relations Authority (FLRA)** is the agency that now administers most of this federal sector bargaining law, performing the same functions that the NLRB does for private sector employees. The FLRA conducts representation elections to determine if a particular group of federal employees wishes to be represented by a labor union, and it investigates and prosecutes allegations of unfair labor practices. The scope of legal rights granted to federal sector unions is more restrictive than those enjoyed by their private sector counterparts. In particular, the types of subjects that these unions have the right to negotiate with federal agencies is much narrower. On the other hand, there are extensive consultation rights on a wide range of topics that federal unions are guaranteed by law. This gives them a foot in the door that is often quite effective in ensuring that the workers' voice is heard.

State and Local Government Employees

Whether particular public sector employees have union rights is determined by whether a state, county or municipality has chosen to enact such a law.

The first state to do so was Wisconsin, in 1959, following increasingly aggressive union organizing in that state by public sector employees. Nearly 40 states now have some form of legislation authorizing unionization by at least some categories of public employees. Many counties and cities similarly provide the right to unionize for some or all of their employees. If you are unionized by virtue of working in one of these jurisdictions, your union and employer operate under a local public sector equivalent of the National Labor Relations Act.

Similar to the legal framework in the federal sector, even for public sector workplaces covered by bargaining legislation, there are always some individuals, such as higher-up managers, who are not eligible for union representation.

Each public sector bargaining law establishes its own definitions for what subjects can be brought up at the bargaining table, what union activities are and are not permitted, and so on. Generally speaking, although a far greater percentage of public sector employees are unionized than their private sector counterparts, public sector unions are more restricted in terms of what they can bargain about, and many do not have the legally protected right to strike. Additionally, union protections for public workers aren't set in stone. Increasingly, hostile political forces work to diminish or eliminate entirely the right to unionize in particular jurisdictions.

Other Workplace Protection Laws

In addition to the basic laws outlining the right to unionize, more and more often many parts of workplace life are regulated by legislation of one sort or another. Learning the exact coverage of these laws can be a pretty complex undertaking, depending on whether you are in the public sector or private sector, working in a particular industry, employed by a large or small company, and many other factors. We won't try to specify an exact listing of which laws apply to you. Rather, here's an idea of what worker protection laws generally cover. Remember, too, that in many instances, you as a union-represented worker enjoy the best of both worlds: the protections of a particular statute, plus your union contract rights. Consult with your union representatives or a lawyer if you spot what may be a violation of your rights.

Here is a quick rundown of the range of subjects covered by workplace legislation and the types of protections such laws contain.

Wages and Hours

The **Fair Labor Standards Act (FLSA)** is the law setting the national minimum wage and standards for overtime pay. Administered by the Department of Labor, this law is far-reaching. Keep in mind, though, that when a state or local law, or of course, your union contract, sets more favorable standards, those will govern. Workplaces must display a poster informing you of your FLSA statutory rights.

According to the government's own calculations, the minimum wage set by federal law is only a fraction of the amount that is needed to live above the poverty level. That's why in dozens of jurisdictions around the country, labor-community coalitions already have succeeded in requiring that, at the local level, a "**living wage**" must be paid.

The FLSA also requires payment at one and one-half times your regular rate of pay for all hours worked beyond 40 in a workweek. This federal law doesn't set any maximum number of hours that can be worked in a day or a week, though, or regulate holiday pay, shift differentials, or anything like that. Any such restrictions or entitlements – and the special pay provisions attached to them – will be found in your union contract or possibly in a state or local statute.

Already weak, the FLSA doesn't cover at all the employment terms of many workers. Complicated rules exempt various employees from its minimum wage and/or overtime requirements, based on type of job worked and on salary level. Those who are in a number of categories like executive and administrative or professional employees (broad groups including teachers in elementary and secondary schools, outside sales employees, and some skilled computer professionals), are not covered by the minimum wage or overtime pay requirements. Other categories of employees (including most farmworkers and live-in domestic service workers) are excluded completely from the overtime pay requirements. In addition, special rules permit a sub-minimum wage for workers who ordinarily earn tips from customers.

Discrimination: Equal Employment Opportunity Commission (EEOC)

Many federal, state and local laws outlaw a number of different kinds of discrimination against both job applicants and current employees. The broadest federal law, formally known as **Title VII of the Civil Rights Act of 1964**, prohibits discrimination based on an employee's race, color, religion, sex, sexual orientation, gender identity, or national origin. Its coverage extends to most private sector employees, plus federal, state and local government workers.

Unlawful discrimination can come up in any aspect of your compensation or your conditions of employment: pay determinations, hiring or firing decisions, promotion or transfer opportunities, or job training and apprenticeship programs. Over the years, legal decisions have established that the scope of what's prohibited is broader than you might realize from just reading the language in the statute. Just a few examples:

•   except under rare circumstances, your employer cannot require that only English be spoken in the workplace.

•   illegal sex discrimination includes workplace sexual harassment

•   the protections of federal law extend to certain forms of discrimination against women who are pregnant. A federal law called the **Pregnancy Discrimination Act** says that your employer can't place any restrictions on use of maternity leave (covering pregnancy, childbirth, and related medical conditions) that aren't also imposed on other uses of disability or sick leave.

These federal antidiscrimination laws are administered by the **Equal Employment Opportunity Commission** (**EEOC**), a government agency with the power to investigate and to bring enforcement actions.

The EEOC also oversees the **Americans with Disabilities Act,** a 1990 federal law. The ADA prohibits discrimination based on an employee's disability, and it requires employers to make reasonable workplace accommodations for a qualified employee with a disability. A counterpart statute, the Rehabilitation Act of 1973, provides very similar protections for federal employees. Both of these statutes cover both physical and mental disabilities.

Another federal statute enforced by the EEOC is the **Equal Pay Act of 1963**. This law requires that women and men receive the same pay for doing "substantially similar" work. This means equal pay for the same type of job. Unfortunately, this law has not been extended to address the big problem of "**comparable worth**"– when women are paid less than men for doing different jobs, but jobs requiring a comparable level of skill and experience. For example, a particular employer may have a higher pay rate for (mostly male) plumbers than for (mostly female) registered nursing assistants, even though the jobs require roughly similar levels of education, degrees of skill and experience, and so on. The same comparison can be made for (mostly male) supermarket stock clerks and (mostly female) cashiers, and lots of other job pairings. Most of the progress in equalizing pay for jobs requiring similar skill and experience levels has been made in union contracts.

Finally, the EEOC enforces the terms of the **Age Discrimination in Employment Act of 1967** (**ADEA**.) This law provides protection against discrimination for those who are 40 years of age or older.

Discrimination: Laws at the Local Level

Every state plus the District of Columbia has its own civil rights law, giving protection to employees – public and private sector – who work in that state. And keep in mind that countless state, county and municipal laws and ordinances add other categories of individuals protected from discriminatory actions. This means that even though the federal laws mentioned above don't bar discrimination based on such factors as marital or parental status, or arrest and conviction records, you may be protected by another law that does.

Business Closings

The 1989 federal **Worker Adjustment and Retraining Notification Act (WARN)** applies to most businesses with 100 or more employees, requiring that they give 60 days advance notice before closing a facility or conducting a mass layoff. Between this federal law and equivalent state laws, each year workers and their families in thousands of workplaces must be given some transition time to adjust to their loss of employment, including obtaining retraining to make it easier to find a new job.

Your union contract probably has provisions that will come into play if there's a shutdown or layoff. These contractual rights go far beyond what the law provides for employees who don't have a union – another instance where being represented gives you two layers of protection.

The WARN law won't stop a company from making business decisions that can cause economic harm to a community. But this law is still a valuable one. As a practical matter, the 60-day "heads up" to a union can provide the time needed to organize community opposition to the company's decision or to apply some other form of pressure to turn it around. This lead time also can enable your union time to work out such accommodations as transfers for employees to other locations that aren't closing, severance pay, and other outstanding issues with pay like saved vacation and sick time.

Family and Medical Leave

As a first step, though not a very big one, in 1993 the **Family and Medical Leave Act (FMLA)** went into effect, intended to provide a means for employees to balance their work and family responsibilities. It does this by saying that workers are legally entitled to take unpaid leave because of any of the following: the birth, care, or adoption or foster care of a child; the care of an immediate family member with a serious health condition; the employee's own serious health condition; or certain military deployments. This law also gives returning employees the right to go back to their old jobs, or to jobs that are nearly identical, without being penalized. The Department of Labor investigates FMLA claims and enforces the terms of the law. The FMLA doesn't cover all workplaces and it requires an employer to grant only unpaid leave (and then only under certain circumstances.) If you're fortunate enough to work in one of the small handful of states that require paid time off, those state rights will trump the relatively weaker protections at the federal level. But your union contract is still the place to look for better provisions than what the law provides. And, as always, the rights that your union has won have priority over inferior provisions in any federal or state law.

The Rights of Veterans and Reservists
A federal law known by the acronym **USERRA** applies to virtually all employers and employees, regardless of size of the employer or the type of job held, or whether the worker is full-time or part-time. And this includes the federal government. Veterans and reservists who served on active duty and who did not receive a dishonorable discharge are entitled to extensive employment and re-employment rights, and are protected against discrimination.

The Department of Labor investigates claims under these laws and has the authority to take appropriate enforcement action. Alternatively, if you've encountered a violation of your rights based on military service, you can seek enforcement directly in court.

Health and Safety
There is a confusing patchwork of laws and agencies that govern workplace health and safety matters, but they're all extremely important. Over five thousand American workers are killed on the job each year, over 50,000 die of occupational disease, and there are millions of workplace injuries and illnesses. The best-known workplace health and safety law is known as **OSHA**, the **Occupational Safety and Health Act**, which is administered by the Department of Labor's **Occupational Safety and Health Administration** (also called OSHA.) Some workplaces, such as those in the coal mining industry, are regulated by a separate

law, and more than half the states administer their own federally approved programs for at least some private and public sector employees. Other laws and federal agencies, such as the **Environmental Protection Agency**, play a role as well. And in all likelihood, your union contract has extra protections for your workplace health and safety.

There are a lot of different sources of rights and responsibilities in this area, but the general standards and principles apply pretty much across the board, covering such things as temperature, air quality, lighting and cleanliness in the

---

Workers Memorial Day

April 28 each year is a day of remembrance and international solidarity. Workers Memorial Day is observed to honor those who have suffered and died on the job and to renew the fight for safe jobs. This observance began in the United States in 1970. But now it's a day when labor unions and their allies in countries around the world stand united, demanding that elected officials put workers' well-being above corporate interests.

---

workplace, exposure to hazardous substances and radiation, and being provided with necessary personal protective equipment, such as respirators, safety goggles and the like. This law and its regulation contain a wealth of detailed requirements for workplace safety. For example, employers are obligated to try to first try to eliminate or reduce hazards before requiring workers to use protective equipment.

Besides all the specific requirements, the federal OSHA law says that employers have a "general duty" to provide work and a workplace free from recognized hazards that are "likely to cause death or serious physical harm." Not surprisingly, unions and employers have a lot of differences about the specifics of what's safe and what isn't. In large part as a result of pressure by unions, OSHA has set specific standards on many particular workplace hazards – exposure to asbestos, rules for working around certain kinds of machinery, and much else – and organized labor is fighting for many more.

As with the Fair Labor Standards Act, workplaces covered by OSHA are required by law to display in a visible place the official OSHA poster that describes everyone's rights and responsibilities under the law. Your steward should be able to answer any questions you may have or to get the needed information from someone more knowledgeable. In fact, your union contract may have established a union health and safety committee, which means that there is already in place a knowledgeable group of individuals to deal with your health and safety concerns. While it's almost always best to work through your union, individuals have the right to contact OSHA or whatever state agency administers your workplace health and safety law to get specific answers about your rights or to file a formal complaint requesting an inspection, usually conducted with no advance notice to the employer, of hazardous conditions. If you do request a workplace inspection, it is possible to have your name withheld from your employer.

In addition to standards for a workplace free of safety and health hazards, you and your union also have the right to information. Your employer is required to maintain, and to keep available for inspection, documentation on workplace hazards. The agencies that administer the law also must furnish you with certain information. Workplace health and safety documents that can be obtained include:

• The Log of Work-Related Injuries and Illnesses, known as OSHA Form 300 (and the summary known as Form 300A.). These contain information on the number of safety and illness incidents at your workplace and time lost due to them. Your employer is required to produce these records for review for at least the past five years.

• Copies of the standards, rules, regulations, and requirements that apply to your workplace, including the OSH Act itself.

• Information on hazardous chemicals as well as relevant employee exposure and medical records, plus information as to what measures the employer is taking to reduce improper exposure levels.

While you need to be very careful in taking this step, under certain conditions, you and your co-workers may also have the right, under the Occupational Safety and Health Act and the National Labor Relations Act, to refuse outright to do unsafe work. To have legal protection for this, the law says that you must have an honest belief that there is an imminent danger of death or serious injury, with the risk being great enough so as to make it impractical to first request an inspection by OSHA or take some other, less drastic step. You will strengthen the legal protection available to you if you are in a position to notify your supervisor before stopping work, and also alert the union and your co-workers beforehand, to enlist their support for collective action. You're best off if you don't refuse the assignment outright; instead, say that you will do the job, once it is made safe.

Finally, there is protection under the law against any reprisal against you if you exercise any of your rights, such as requesting a workplace inspection or access to relevant records, or even just complaining to your employer.

The problem with health and safety laws is the same as for many other legal protections: what the law says is one thing, but the enforcing agency's practical ability to enforce the law can be quite another. For example, current funding levels would permit the federal enforcement agency to inspect individual workplaces for hazards only once every 160 years or so, and federal and state staffing levels provide for about one inspector for every 70,000+ employees. The obvious result? Lots and lots of workplaces are out of compliance with the law on an ongoing basis.

Whistleblowing

A "**whistleblower**" is an employee who gives information to the public, the news media, or a government agency about some employer activity that is illegal or improper in some way. Because the disclosure of information about corruption, cost overruns, or production of defective or harmful products can seriously damage an employer, you often see retaliation against whistleblowers.

But the U.S. Constitution and many federal, state and local laws provide protection for at least some people who blow the whistle. Since the stakes are often high, be very cautious if you are thinking of going public with sensitive information. Don't go around chatting with those who don't have a need to know. As a general rule, if you don't want what you say to be on the front page of the New York Times, don't say it, or type it for that matter. It's wise to consult in confidence only with a union officer or with an attorney of your choosing for expert guidance on the best and safest way to get out the information you have.

ERISA: Federal Pension Law

Laws written, not coincidentally by lawyers, can be pretty fearsome and complicated creatures. But the law that governs virtually all private employer-provided pension and retirement benefit plans, known as **ERISA**, probably wins the prize for "Most Difficult to Understand by a Normal Human Being." When it was passed, ERISA quickly gained the sarcastic nickname, "The Full Employment Act for Lawyers."

What is easy to understand is that ERISA provides two important types of protections for those with what are known as "**defined benefit**" pension plans. These are the older types of pension plans, where the dollar amount of your eventual pension payments is based on your years of employment and earnings, as opposed to "**defined contribution**" plans, where contributions are made to an individual IRA-type fund. There are substantive rights, such as requirements for when an employee must be able to vest, meaning how many years must be worked before being eligible for a pension.

ERISA also regulates employer-provided health plans, including what's known as the **COBRA** right to continue coverage under your health insurance after your employment ends. And it contains many procedural protections for employees. For example, it requires that a claims procedure be in place and that a great deal of information about the employer's plans and your coverage be made available.

Immigration

The battle over what place immigrant workers have in the U.S. is a hugely important one for American unions. Immigration is fueled by the fact that for many people and families, coming to the United States offers the only hope for a life free of violence and poverty. Their motivation is no different than that of many American families who came to this country generations ago.

Forces hostile to the interests of working people have succeeded in putting in place a legal structure that makes it an uphill battle for immigrants to work honestly and productively in exchange for a living wage. The key tool that employers use is fear; relying on the fact that immigrant workers are constantly in legal jeopardy and are living in an inhospitable political environment. Because of this uncertainty and fear, some employers boldly subject immigrant workers to wage

> ### "All of Us Are Immigrants" (Steve Earle, songwriter and activist)
>
> Virtually every American worker is from a family that immigrated to the U.S. at some point in the recent or distant past. So it stands to reason that unions are in the forefront of advocacy work in legislatures and communities to advance and protect the rights of immigrant workers. In addition, many unions offer direct assistance in a variety of ways. Union programs offer legal advice and counseling, workshops and application preparation to help members apply for United States citizenship, classes to teach English as a Second Language, and U.S. History, Government and Civics classes to prepare immigrant workers for their citizenship interviews and exams.

theft and to deplorable health and safety conditions without consequences, since those workers understandably fear retaliation if they challenge those conditions.

Historically, employers have relied on divide and conquer strategies, pitting one group against another. Sometimes this is along racial or ethnic lines, encouraging workers to resist the effort by others to gain a foothold in the workplace. Sometimes it's encouraging men to push back against women seeking equality in the workplace. And in the case of immigrant workers, there's a long history in the U.S. of native-born workers viewing immigrants as threats. Sad to say, this is part of a worldwide phenomenon, as we witness the rise of nationalism.

But unions understand that in solidarity lies our strength. If everyone in the workplace rejects the idea of division and stands together, this is the most powerful counterweight to employers' ability to underpay and exploit workers. Today, millions of immigrants are active dues paying union members, and union contracts play a vital role in strengthening the legal protections available to all workers, regardless of immigration or citizenship status.

Take for example the **Immigration Reform and Control Act (IRCA)**, which is the federal law dealing with employers hiring workers who are not U.S. citizens. To control the hiring of undocumented workers, this law sets forth requirements as to what personal identification documents your employer can insist upon seeing, and when. But since many employers don't respect the restrictions that these laws place on the process, union contracts spell out what is and is not permitted. This educates workers on their rights and defines limits on what employers can get away with. Additionally, it provides an enforcement mechanism if the immigrant workers' rights aren't respected. Along similar lines, your union contract may obligate your employer to refuse to allow federal immigration officers to enter the workplace unless they have a warrant.

The fact of the matter is, almost all of the law's protections that are discussed in this chapter apply to all workers, including immigrants: to form and be active in a union; to be free from workplace discrimination; to work under healthy and safe conditions; to have employers accommodate disabilities, and much more.

Polygraph Tests

With very limited exceptions, the **Employee Polygraph Protection Act** prohibits most private sector employers from requiring either applicants or current employees to take lie detector tests. And even when these tests are permitted, the law sets strict guidelines for how they are to be administered.

Workers' Compensation

Most American workers are now covered by federal and state workers' compensation laws. But there are exceptions, such as those working in the freelance "gig" economy, domestic workers and farmworkers. This is an automatic type of insurance program, based on a no-fault concept: if you are injured or disabled in connection with your job, you receive a set payment for your loss and reimbursement for any medical expenses, and you are eligible for weekly disability payments.

Workers' compensation is a mixed blessing for workers. On the one hand, the uniform laws and set schedules for payment increase the chances of getting mandatory compensation for your injury or illness, and can cut down on the need for time-consuming and expensive litigation. On the other hand, these laws take away your right to sue your employer for negligence and to recover damages for pain and suffering. This means that you may not be able to receive the amount of compensation that you truly deserve.

Time limits are extremely important in pursuing some of your rights under workers' compensation laws, so consult with your union steward immediately if you're hurt or become ill on the job. When in doubt about whether your condition is work-related, ask questions. You may learn for instance, the law covers even some injuries that occur during your commute to or from work.

Privacy

Monitoring of employees has become a bedrock feature of the American workplace. It's estimated that half of U.S. employers have a video monitoring program in place, and two-thirds conduct surveillance of workplace email use.

Some state laws restrict monitoring in various ways, such as prohibiting employers from demanding user names and passwords that employees use on social media sites. At the federal level, the 1986 **Electronic Communications Privacy Act of 1986 (ECPA)** is the only law that provides any employee protection. Unfortunately, that protection is quite limited. ECPA permits employers to monitor various communications, including email sent and received on employer email systems, as well as phone calls, so long as personal communications are not included. This means, for example, that an employer listening in to calls made by sales representatives must stop listening if it becomes apparent that a particular call is a personal one. And in most jurisdictions there are no prohibitions against a host of other types of monitoring, such as using GPS in employer-owned vehicles or cell phone tracking in company-issued phones to keep track of employees' whereabouts.

But employer monitoring of employee communications and use of social media outside the workplace may also run afoul of other federal or state laws. Suppose an employer checks an employee's posts on social media and learns that the employee is in a category protected by anti-discrimination laws (race, age, sex, and so on). It may well have been legal for the employer to have looked at the employee's social media activity. But it would be illegal to then discriminate against the employee based on the protected group status, that the employer would not have known about if it hadn't been for the social media monitoring. Similarly, if employer monitoring reveals that an employee is exercising the right to speak up about working conditions, any discrimination or retaliation that followed could then provide grounds for an unfair labor practice charge.

In unionized workplaces, of course, the limited legal protections that workers have are often expanded by specific provisions in collective bargaining agreements. So to understand the full range of any legal protections, you need to factor in (1) the federal law, (2) any workplace privacy law that your state may have, and (3) what your union has won through bargaining.

IF YOU GET IN

trouble

Whether you're "innocent" or "guilty," one day you may find yourself called into your supervisor's office to answer questions. The grilling may be about an alleged problem with your job performance. Or it may be about serious misconduct, like an accusation that you've stolen property from work or cheated on a timesheet.

Your first thought may be, "I haven't done anything wrong" or "I haven't done anything different than what folks do around here all the time, so there's no harm in answering a few questions." But many workers (like many criminal defendants) find themselves in hot water when an over-eager supervisor or company investigator deliberately twists perfectly innocent answers to questions or takes answers out of context to create a misleading impression. So better safe than sorry; educate yourself now about your basic rights in this area, so you can use them if you have to.

Unfortunately, in the workplace we don't have all the rights that we saw growing up when we watched someone in a movie or on TV getting questioned by the police. There's no workplace equivalent of the Miranda right to remain silent, or even notification of the right to have a lawyer (or union steward, in your case) present. If you're asked questions about a work-related matter, you do have to give answers.

But you can – and should – provide yourself with the protection you will have if a union representative is present:

• your steward can learn beforehand what the questioning is going to be about;

• you can consult with your steward privately before the questioning starts;

• your steward can keep a written record of the meeting and serve as a witness afterward about what you said; and

• your steward can offer additional information for the employer to consider, and make sure the questioning stays within reasonable bounds.

Your rights to union representation are known as "**Weingarten Rights**," after a 1975 U.S. Supreme Court ruling. As labor-friendly and labor-unfriendly majorities have switched at the National Labor Relations Board, sometimes these rights have applied only to unionized workers in the private sector, and sometimes to all private sector workers. Through legislation and subsequent court decisions, these basic protections are now generally extended to federal employees, as well as to many state and local government workers.

Under Weingarten you have the legal right to have a union representative (but not necessarily a lawyer) present during a meeting with the management if ALL of the following conditions are met:

1. *The meeting is an investigatory interview.* This means that you are expected to answer questions in connection with an inquiry into possible wrong-doing or unacceptable behavior. Weingarten rights do not cover meetings where the communication is one-way; that is, when the purpose is merely to convey information to you or to notify you of a decision already made regarding discipline.

2. *Disciplinary action may result from the meeting.* The law requires only that disciplinary action of *any* severity is one possible result of the meeting.

3. *You "reasonably believe" that disciplinary action may result.* If there is a legal dispute over whether your concern about possible disciplinary action is "reasonable," the determination will be made based on all the circumstances

surrounding the meeting: has your supervisor previously raised the possibility of discipline? Have other employees already been disciplined for what you're accused of? Are you already working under the threat of a performance warning letter?

4. *You make a request for representation.* This is another way Weingarten rights differ from Miranda rights: your employer generally is under no obligation to inform you of your right to be represented. It's up to you to know your rights, and to assert them.

So here's some practical advice if a supervisor wants to ask you questions about something on the job:

1. *Ask what the meeting will be about.* If the answer confirms that the employer is indeed looking into something of a disciplinary nature, then insist on having a union representative present. You should say something along the following lines: "Since it seems to me that this meeting might lead to a disciplinary action being taken against me, I request that my union representative be present. If you will not allow this, I will respectfully decline to answer any questions unless you order me to do so." If it's not clear at first whether you might end up being disciplined, ask if there is "any possibility" that disciplinary action may result. If you get any answer besides a clear "no," then insist on having a union representative present before going any further. If someone isn't available then and there, ask for the meeting to be rescheduled for a time when a representative can be there. It's your right.

2. *If your request for representation is denied, think twice before you refuse to answer questions.* It's risky to do that, since you then face the possibility of being disciplined for not answering work-related questions. Instead, it's usually wiser to make it clear that you will answer questions only if you are directed to do so. After proceeding under protest, you can consult your union steward about the best way to then challenge the denial of representation, including by filing an unfair labor practice charge.

Protection from Retaliation

It's easy enough for legislators to pass laws establishing workplace rights. And it's easy for you to read about them in this book. But everybody knows that in the Real World, it sometimes takes more than a little bit of courage to exercise your rights. Everyone has seen examples, in the workplace and outside of it, where an individual speaking up then has to deal with the consequences of having made someone in a position of power unhappy.

If you are faced with making a decision about whether to assert your rights, or to just go on with things the way they are, there are few important considerations to keep in mind.

First, there are many legal protections available to both private and public sector employees who speak up and invoke their rights. Section 7 of the National Labor Relations Act (see pages 108-113) specifically sets forth legal protection against retaliation for those who speak or act with their co-workers to deal with their working conditions. Any retaliation by your employer can usually be challenged by filing an unfair labor practice charge with the NLRB or with your state labor board. And remember that most of the laws discussed in this and the preceding chapter have their own provisions that make it illegal for your employer to retaliate against you in any way for exercising rights under that particular statute, including protection if you file a charge or complaint. Suppose, for example, you pursue a discrimination action, alleging that you were denied a promotion based on your race. After you've filed the charge, you find yourself moved to a lousy shift in a sister location seventy-five miles from your home. It may turn out in the end that even if you don't have enough proof to overturn the decision to deny you the promotion, you may still be able to get your shift and work location restored because that employer action will be found to be retaliation for your having filed the initial charge.

Risky, But Worth It

Be aware that there can be a difference between what you know actually occurred and what you can prove as a matter of law. You'd be kidding yourself if you thought that there's never been an instance in which a worker was retaliated against for having engaged in behavior that is legally protected but was unable to prove that the retaliation took place. Still, don't let this prevent you from asserting your rights. There have been more instances where the agency charged with enforcing a law moved aggressively against an employer trying to prevent an employee from asserting rights under that law. After all, if all employees are successfully intimidated into not using the provisions of the law, that agency becomes useless. Be sure to remember your double layer of union protection: reprisals can be defended against through the grievance/arbitration procedure in a good number of union contracts.

Also remember that, just as in all other aspects of life, there can be no forward progress without some degree of risk taking. True, you may be opening yourself up to some new problems on the job if you take action against existing problems. But if you do nothing, the two most likely outcomes are (1) the current problems will remain, or (2) the current problems will just get worse.

THE

union's face

OUTSIDE THE WORKPLACE

We've taken a look at how your union is set up and how it functions inside the workplace. But to paint a more complete picture of what unions are and what they do, let's turn to the broader labor union agenda in two critical areas: organizing and politics.

The Challenges of Organizing

Most union members probably don't have a very good idea of what went into changing their place of work from non-union to union. Almost all current union members were hired into an already represented workplace, and played no role in establishing the union. It would be a mistake, though, to assume that those who did had an easy time of it.

At different points in the history of American unions, organizing activity took place at varying levels of intensity. Depending on how aggressively unions were organizing, and because of changes elsewhere in society, the total percentage of union membership has changed dramatically over the years. Organizing among some types of employees – notably government workers–has been steadily increasing for many years now. Thanks partly to a significantly higher victory rate in public sector union elections than in those in the private sector, close to half of organized labor now consists of government employees. And since in many ways the political and legal obstacles to union organizing are much lower in the public than in the private sector, the rate of new union organizing in the former is more than five times higher than in the latter. But despite the vigorous growth of public sector unionism, overall the percentage of the American workforce that is unionized has declined since its peak many decades ago.

The early decades of union organizing in the United States involved private sector workplaces, where union organizing has always been a rougher ride than in the public sector. The pioneers of unionization in the private sector frequently encountered employers who responded to organizing drives with physical violence. Many of the early industrial unions got their footholds only by standing up to a court system that jailed union supporters and to the clubs and guns of company thugs. Sometimes the bullets that maimed and killed union supporters and their families were fired by state militias or federal troops serving as private armies for anti-union employers.

In the decades since, we've moved on to less obviously aggressive forms of resistance to union organizing drives in the private sector. But even if your workplace was organized in the post-World War II era, it is quite likely that your predecessors had to stand up to significant attempts by your employer to intimidate union supporters. While those who came before you may not have had to dodge company bullets, they did have to maintain the courage of their convictions to stand together in the face of modern-day employer responses to organizing drives that include:

- illegal threats to shut down if the workplace is organized; a threat that is made in well over half of recent union organizing drives;
- illegal threats to cut wages or benefits if workers choose union representation, a threat made in almost half of all organizing drives;
- illegally firing employees who decide to become actively involved in organizing drives; something that takes place in more than one third of all organizing drives;
- interrogating workers in mandatory one-on-one meetings with their supervisors about support for the union ; used in almost two-thirds of organizing drives.

Paying the Price – in Blood

Organizers and activists face considerable pressure these days to abandon their efforts to band together in their unions. But for victories in worker organizing in the early years, there was often a price paid in blood.

In 1914, members of the United Mine Workers of America in Ludlow, Colorado went out on strike against a company that was part of the Rockefeller industrial empire. As was routine in those days, the company promptly evicted the miners and their families from the company-owned housing. So the mining families set up a tent colony, which then was surrounded by the National Guard.

As the strike wore on, sometimes at night the militia would shoot their rifles into the colony. For greater protection, the miners dug a cave inside the largest tent, where they moved their family members who were among them.

On Easter night, while the miners and their families were asleep, company thugs and members of the National Guard poured oil on the strikers' tents and set the tents ablaze. As the men, women, and children ran from the inferno, they were machine-gunned.

The death toll – the price paid for seeking a better life through a union – was over a dozen of the children and wives of the miners. The strikers themselves were placed on a blacklist, preventing them from holding jobs in the coal industry.

And how did the courts deal with what became known as the Ludlow Massacre? Scores of the miners and their union leaders were placed under arrest. Of Rockefeller and the other owners, the detective agency brought in to suppress the strike, and the state militia who fired into the tents, not a single one was brought to justice.

But although the Ludlow strikers didn't get their union recognized, the story didn't end there. Fellow mine workers and members of other unions in Colorado attacked scabs at other mines. Rockefeller himself was hounded, including by a minister who protested in front of a New York church that Rockefeller attended. (The minister was beaten by police). It took some time, and more deaths, but the United Mine Workers succeeded in establishing a strong union presence in the western mine industry.

And once the union comes in, one battle may be over but the war is far from won. The goal of the union, of course, is not just winning representation rights. What the workers need is to get a collective bargaining agreement in place. It's the union contract that establishes workplace rights and provides a way to enforce those rights. But far too often, the employer's resistance to union representation continues even after the workers get their union. In more than half of newly organized private sector workplaces, employers successfully use stall and delay tactics to prevent the union from securing a collective bargaining agreement in the first year.

"How Low Can You Go?"

Sometimes employers pull out all the stops to keep out unions, but the workers succeed in gaining union representation anyway. A handful of employers have earned a reputation as carrying on the anti-union fight to the bitter end, no matter what. Walmart may be the best (worst?) example in the United States.

The United Food and Commercial Workers succeeded in getting a foothold at the aggressively anti-union Walmart by winning a union election in the meat-cutting department at a Walmart store in Jacksonville, Texas. There weren't a whole lot of jobs at stake here: the vote was 7 in favor of union representation, 3 against. But the company wasn't the least bit gracious in defeat. They thought about their options, and figured that if they shut down the meat-cutting department at that store in Texas, that would look like illegal retaliation against that group of workers having voted for the union. So instead, 11 days after the union vote, Walmart shut down every meat-cutting department in every Walmart store in the United States!

It doesn't have to be this way. The American labor law system could provide a fair way for the majority of American workers who say they would want to be in a union to bring that about. And in large part, we see how this could work by comparing the private sector to the public sector. Despite an increase in hostility towards public sector unionism, public workers who want to unionize still face far less formidable obstacles. As a result, the win rate for government workers is much higher, and it's much easier for their unions to achieve first contracts.

Of course, many states don't even have a legal framework for organizing by government workers. But in jurisdictions where unionization is legally protected, public sector employers are far more hands off than private employers. Sometimes, the employer mounts no campaign at all to resist an organizing drive. The decision as to whether or not to unionize is left entirely in the hands of the workers themselves, as it should be. And even when public sectors employer do use some of the same tactics to resist unionization, the intensity is often less severe.

Digital Organizing

The fundamentals of what's broadly referred to as "organizing" – finding out what workers' concerns are, educating workers as to what a union is and how union representation can help improve the workplace, and employees discussing things among themselves – are the same as they always have been in the union world. What's different now is the technology, and how it can facilitate communication.

You've likely seen the power of digital media and how it can mobilize groups of people around a common cause. Not surprisingly, unions increasingly are using the tools of digital organizing: social media and mobile devices make it easier to connect and share information, and to mobilize people. Digital tools are used by unions to sign workers up as members, to bring them together for union meetings and public events, and to stimulate the back and forth conversation that's needed to find the best ways to move forward. A good example of one union that's taken to this in a big way is the International Association of Fire Fighters. That union has more than 225,000 "likes" on Facebook, which is more than two-thirds of their membership! Many unions now use social media effectively as a way of contacting and mobilizing *potential* union members and quickly sharing information together. Non-union workers can share stories instantly of injustices they face on the job, illegal handbills and threats from managers, all empowering their fight and helping garnish support to unionize.

Also contributing to the relative ease of organizing government workers is the fact that in some jurisdictions, a much easier path to union recognition is possible. In the private sector nowadays, virtually all organizing drives involve winning an election supervised by the National Labor Relations Board. The time it takes to get to that election allows employers to mount their anti-union campaigns of intimidation. In contrast, some states and localities provide for what's called "card check." Instead of having to go through the election process, unions simply have to demonstrate that they have the support of a majority of the workers who would be covered by a collective bargaining agreement. That's usually done by having individuals sign cards confirming that they want to be union-represented. Once the neutral labor board checks those signatures, the union is certified as the bargaining representative. Critics of card check argue that a secret ballot election is more democratic. But they ignore the fact that the bottom line in card check is that a majority of all those affected – rather than a majority of those who show up to vote in an election – determines the group's future.

Why Support New Organizing?

Working in a unionized workplace, you may think that it doesn't make much of a difference to you how much new union organizing is going on elsewhere. You may even be uncomfortable with the fact that part of your hard-earned dues dollars are devoted to winning union protection and workplace rights for others, rather than being spent on negotiations and representation in your own workplace. But there are good reasons why supporting union efforts to organize the unorganized and to help unorganized workers improve their working lives makes sense, not just for other workers who need help, but for you, too.

Immediate Gain

Every day, in some direct or indirect way, you experience the benefits of unionization. Today may or may not be the day that the discipline provision in your contract saves your job, or that union enforcement of health and safety standards prevents you from being injured, or that you are able to get the day off *with pay* to care for your sick child. But even if something this apparent does not take place, for almost all workers, today is the day that you earn more money than you would have without a union – and have better health coverage and other benefits. Many statistical studies have documented the dollars-and-cents difference that union membership contributes to. Annual statistics published by the U.S. Department of Labor show that unionized workers on average earned over 20 percent more than non-union workers (and interestingly, this "union premium" has held steady since the 1930's), and that:

- unionized women similarly earned over 25 percent more than non-union women;

- unionized Latinos earned over 40 percent more than non-union Latinos; and

- unionized African-Americans earned close to 25 percent more than non-union African-Americans.

> ### "How Many Dollars in My Pocket?"
>
> The effect of the "union premium" over a worker's lifetime can add up to quite a bit of money.
>
> Take the cases of two more or less average workers at the beginning of their working lives. One is lucky enough to be union-represented, and the other is not. Using data from the U.S. Department of Labor's Bureau of Labor Statistics, you can calculate that the union worker can expect to be $551,000 wealthier on retirement day. In some industries, the differential is even higher. Construction workers who are not unionized are effectively losing out on $1.1 million in earnings over the course of their careers!

And for workers just starting out, the union advantage is crystal clear as well, with younger unionized workers earning over 29 percent more than their non-union counterparts.

So there's no question that your quality of life is better because you are union-represented. Given that, it's simply the right thing to do to help others gain that same level of rewards for their hard work. We make society better for all when each of us makes a personal decision to pitch in and help others acquire what we already have.

Protecting What We've Won

Even if what you are most focused on is conditions in your own workplace, here's something to consider: successful union organizing in other workplaces will improve things for you.

How much clout your union has at the bargaining table and in the legislative arena and elsewhere often is determined by "**union density**." This term refers to the degree to which employees in your particular industry or geographic area are unionized. Simply stated, the greater the percentage of employees who are unionized, the more power each union has to win and enforce good contracts and to be an influential part of the process to enact a labor-friendly legislative agenda. Many statistical studies have shown that unions are better able to negotiate higher wages for the employees they represent when the employees of employers in the same competitive market are organized.

Additionally, studies have demonstrated that higher union density also benefits nonunion workers, by significantly raising their pay. This is mostly a result of two factors: (1) employers' efforts to keep their wages competitive, so as not to lose workers to unionized shops, and (2) employers' trying to make sure that their employees have less of an incentive to organize.

Learning From Mickey Mouse

One clear example of how the strength of unionized workers can benefit unrepresented workers is the hospitality industry in Orlando, Florida. Negotiations between a coalition of six local unions and Disney World raised the minimum starting wage in the union contract covering housekeepers, lifeguards, cast members, and other service workers. Disney then extended the raises to all 70,000 of its Orlando employees, even though only half were unionized. Like dominos falling, SeaWorld Orlando and other companies in Orlando's hospitality and retail sector raised wages for all of *their* nonunionized workers, as well.

Reducing Inequality

Economic studies of unions and their effect on Americans' financial wellbeing have led to an inescapable conclusion: the increases we've seen in economic inequality are directly related to the decline in unionization. If anyone tells you that the reason American workers' earnings have gone down is that we just don't work hard enough, point out that over the course of the decades since 1973, the hourly compensation of a typical American blue collar manufacturing worker has remained close to unchanged, rising by just 12.4 percent after inflation. But during that same time period, productivity increased 77 percent!

Unions Are the Rising Tide (That Lifts All Boats)

The history of capitalism in the U.S. is full of examples of the various strategies that companies adopt to resist unionization by their workers. Some use aggressive tactics, while others adopt a more subtle, creative approach: they raise workplace standards for nonunion workers just enough to dampen any enthusiasm those workers might have for unionizing.

One excellent historical example of this is the policies adopted by Kodak in Rochester, NY. Here was a company operating in a heavily unionized part of the country, where many in the workforce had neighbors and relatives enjoying the better wages and benefits and increased job security that come with union representation. In order to head off any potential organizing drive at Kodak, management there paid a sizable "wage dividend." Kodak increased pay rates to make them comparable to union levels, and also offered decent benefits, including paid vacations and a solid pension plan, and even provided lots of extra perks, like recreational programs. The company gave its workers the kind of job security that usually is enjoyed only in a union shop, where members have the protections of the "just cause" standard that's required before any discipline is meted out.

Your Role in Organizing

If you're persuaded about the importance of your union's external organizing efforts, you probably are glad that you're making a financial contribution toward that effort, whether that's done through part of your union dues, or perhaps a special assessment for an organizing fund. But you're not off the hook just yet. As with many other areas of the day-to-day work of the union, it's not enough to pay your money and let "the union" take care of doing the work.

There are two reasons for you to become personally involved in organizing activity outside of your workplace. First, a healthy, democratic, effective union is one in which the members pitch in to do the work, greatly increasing the people-resources of the union. Second, no matter how skilled professional union staffers may be – even assuming your union has them – there is an extra measure of credibility when an already-organized employee speaks directly to an unorganized worker about day-to-day experiences on the job. The successes of member-to-member organizing are clear. Studies document that unions are far more successful in winning bargaining rights in organizing drives conducted by ordinary members rather than by professional staff. It makes perfect sense; people want to hear it from the source, from someone who has been in their shoes.

The Importance of Politics

There are legal limitations on the right of unions to use regular members' dues to make financial contributions in an election. For that reason, your union may have a political action committee, or PAC, funded with non-dues dollars voluntarily contributed by members. And certainly at the local level or above, your union is likely to be involved in trying to influence the workings of mayors, governors and other elected officials. Why so much emphasis on political action?

Aside and apart from getting worker-friendly elected officials into office, unions play a critical role for all in society when they advocate on behalf of their members, and indeed, all working people. At the federal level, unions are an organized voice for preserving the fundamental right of workers to choose to have a union. They advocate for stronger health and safety and other workplace protections for all workers. Simply put, while other organizations and politicians may forget about workers, the well being of working men and women is a union's first and only concern at all levels of government. At the state and local level, unions are in the forefront of the fight on a broad range of issues decided in each city, county, or state – things like wage theft, expanding protections against discrimination, minimum wage, paid family leave. Again, these are issues that affect not only unionized workers, but the community as a whole.

That's why most unions have a vigorous political action and organizing operation. Some of this work is done by elected leaders and staff. They research the issues to analyze how potential legislation might affect unionized workplaces and the society at large. They establish and develop connections with legislators to make sure they are aware of the issues and concerns of workers and the impact their votes on legislation will have on workers and their livelihoods. But a big share of the work done on legislative issues is carried out directly by rank and file union members. Your union may have an annual Lobby Day, for example, when droves of members flood the halls of the legislature to make sure that elected representatives understand *our* view on the votes to be taken. And union members are enlisted to speak to neighbors and community groups, again to make sure that the interests of workers and our communities are factored into each political decision that's made. Just as mentioned above how members make more of an impact speaking to workers interested in organizing, the same goes here. Politicians want to hear from union members more than they want to hear from the staff. Union members are the blood of the community; they are the constituents and the backbone of their base.

Money and Politics

When it comes to political contributions, the playing field for unions and for businesses is far from a level one, though. For years, unions have been badly outspent by the wealthiest Americans, and the gap is widening. All of this was blown wide open with the 2010 decision by the U.S. Supreme Court in the ***Citizens United*** case. That ruling stated – hang on here – (1) that corporations are people, and are therefore entitled to the same free speech protections as other "people"; (2) that spending money is a form of legally protected "free speech"; and (3) that under the First Amendment, campaign contributions by corporations and unions therefore can't legally be restricted. The claim that this is fair, since both unions and corporations are subject to the identical rules, brings to mind the observation by Anatole France, "In its majestic equality, the law forbids rich and poor alike to sleep under bridges, beg in the streets and steal loaves of bread." Since that *Citizens United* ruling, a billion dollars has been spent on political "speech" with no way of knowing who's behind the funding.

And the problem is compounded by the tremendous imbalance between the wealthy who use "dark money" – political spending with undisclosed donors – and other types of funding to finance antiunion and other pro-business campaigns. Using Super PACS and other ways of avoiding both disclosures and taxes, wealthy corporations and individuals are badly outspending unions and legitimate public interest groups. Despite all the propaganda about "big union money", the fact is that the funding network put together by the anti-union Koch brothers alone spends several times more on political contributions than the 10 largest U.S. union contributors.

Over the years, most unions have learned that if they try to compete for political influence with business on the dollar-for-dollar basis, the interests of working people come up short. The bottom line is that those pursuing businesses' political interests simply have far more money than workers and our allies do. So as important as it is for union members to provide financial support for labor-friendly politicians, other ways of exerting political influence are needed, too. The story is told of a labor delegation that went to lobby President Franklin Roosevelt after his 1932 election. The unionists promptly launched into arguments for pro-labor policies. But what Roosevelt needed was not convincing, but to know that he would have the political clout to push such legislation through Congress. His response to the labor leaders: "I agree with you. I want to do it. Now go out and make me do it." That's still the way our political system works: if we want worker-friendly policies, we've got to create the political pressure to bring that about.

The pro-worker New Deal legislation that Roosevelt was able to get passed – thanks in large part to union mobilization – is an example of the success of union political clout. And there certainly have been numerous positive examples since, like the ever-expanding protections against discrimination on the job. At the same time, we need to recognize that other needed improvements in the law, like strengthening the protections granted to union organizing, haven't been as successful because unions and their members haven't brought sufficient pressure to bear. Our lobbying and agitation pay off!

Elect the Boss Why should *you* care about your union's involvement in the world of politics? As is the case with new union organizing, what your union does on the political landscape has very direct impact on your union's effectiveness in your and other workplaces. Perhaps the most dramatic example of the direct connection between the political arena and the world of collective bargaining is the situation in which public employees find themselves. It is not an oversimplification to say that public employees get to "elect the boss" when they get involved in electoral campaigns and in how politicians subsequently carry out their duties. It would be throwing away a critical source of leverage if a public employee union did not strive to have influence over who their elected government officials will be and how those officials pass legislation and govern day-to-day. It's those officials who directly determine how much money is budgeted for union members' salaries, pensions and other benefits, whether or not to contract out public employees' jobs, and much more. This is why public sector union members are often in the forefront of the GOTV ("get out the vote") efforts designed to mobilize working people and their allies to show up on election day to help produce the right results.

Influence Inside and Outside the Workplace

And for every employee, both those in the public sector and those in the private sector, what goes on in the world of politics has a direct connection to the union's ability to advance and protect the members' interests. Legislatures pass and enforce laws that can make it easier or harder for unions to organize, to protect members' health and safety , to have reasonable health care coverage, and to improve countless other aspects of working life. What is won at a bargaining table can be taken away with a stroke of a pen by elected officials, or by appointed or elected judges who are not worker-friendly. Public workers see this all too clearly when they succeed in winning solid pay raises or pension benefits in negotiations, but then watch as legislatures refuse to provide the funding needed to make these things happen. And lots of unions got an unpleasant look at this in action when the U.S. Supreme Court ruled that lifetime health care benefits negotiated for retirees in fact expire at the end of each collective bargaining agreement.

145

On an even broader scale, the priorities that are set by our elected leaders determine in large part what resources will be available to us as organized workers. Consider that fact that the U.S. now spends far more on prisons and jails than on public higher education. California, for example, spends close to $80,000 a year for each inmate, but just a bit over $11,000 to educate each K-12 student. The impact of this goes far beyond how it affects unionized employees on campuses. Think about what it means when our society decides to spend more on prisons than schools. When this is the case, what are the prospects for those of us who would like to be able to send our kids to get a good college education, with tuition that is affordable?

If you're not convinced your union should be involved in politics, the question is, if unions don't lobby for workplace health and safety laws, or for living wages, then who will?

your role

IN YOUR UNION

In any society, each individual has to make a fundamental decision about how to relate to the larger group. Some end up not taking very seriously the degree to which their participation in group decision-making and action can make a difference. Whether it's because of the crunch of a million other things every day or some other reason, many people don't put much time into educating themselves as to what is going on. We don't end up spending much time reading a daily newspaper or watching the TV news or keeping up on current events on line, we don't always vote in elections, and don't join the PTA or get directly involved in our kids' schooling. It's easy to get caught up and distracted like this, but it's also easy to make an impact. All of us are directly affected by the decisions that elected government officials make, the quality of public education, and lots of other things that we haven't been directly involved in.

There is another approach, of course, to involvement in society: realizing that when we as individuals educate ourselves as to what is going on around us, and the more we actively participate in shaping the future, we are all better off. This is not to say that our society is a perfectly functioning democracy. All too often policies are set and actions carried out based more on who has the money or power than on what the majority of people really think. But the more that individuals choose to opt out of the decisions that are made, the less democratic things become, and the less our society reflects what most people really want.

The decisions you have to make as an individual represented by a union are really no different from the decisions you make regarding the broader issues in society. You might not place a high priority on keeping informed about issues in your workplace and the actions taken by your labor representative, and you may have only limited participation in the daily life of the union. But then, just as with what happens in the larger society, for better or worse you're stuck with whatever is decided by the folks who are running the union and the decisions they make. But there is an alternative: since your union is nothing more than a collection of individual members, you can choose to become actively involved, and in so doing shape what your union is and what it does.

So if you want to "own" your union, and to share in the members' responsibility of running it, what can you do?

Educate Yourself

As the saying goes, "no investigation, no right to speak." If you're going to participate in the union decisions that affect your workplace life, you should do so intelligently. This means taking the time to learn about the union and the issues it is dealing with on behalf of the members. If you don't have access to a copy of the union contract, make an effort to find it online, or get a print copy and look through it, at least enough to get a good idea about what topics are covered and what some of the specifics are. Make a mental note not only of what rights the union is already in a position to protect but also what improvements you'd like to see in the next round of bargaining.

Your union probably puts out one or more electronic or print newsletters, magazines, or newspapers designed to fill members in on the issues of the day. National unions and a strong majority of locals have websites with up to date information about union activities and issues, and many have a social media presence that is constantly updated as news breaks. Treat these like your daily newspaper: you certainly don't have to read every word, but devoting just a little bit of time can yield a lot of useful information. Most unions also have print publications or online information on specific topics, such as explaining your health and safety rights, the union's political action program, and so on. Get familiar with your union website and find out from your steward what resources are available to learn what you need to know.

Your union holds periodic meetings open to all members, as well as business meetings of leadership bodies that you might check out as an observer. At the local, regional, or national level, there may be workshops or training programs that you can attend to learn about specific topics. Often, these programs are presented at no or minimal cost to interested members.

If you're going to participate in the workings of your union, it's probably not a bad idea to check out the union's constitution and bylaws. These documents will specify when and how union meetings and elections are conducted, what committees and other structures the union uses to do its work, and what rights members have to participate in such matters as ratification votes on a new collective bargaining agreement.

In the process of trying to learn more about your union and what it does, you will undoubtedly have lots of questions. Your union steward is a Jack or Jane of All Trades, with a job description that's pretty lengthy, but first on the list should be helping members understand the union's actions. So don't hesitate to insist on answers that will make you a better-informed "union citizen."

Be a Set of "Eyes and Ears"

The first instruction given to new union stewards is that they need to be the "eyes and ears" of the union in the workplace. A union contract isn't worth the paper it's printed on if its terms aren't enforced by the union when the employer is in violation. But "the union" can't take any action unless it knows what the facts are. It's union stewards who serve as fact gatherers who can report what's going on to others with responsibility for putting together the right responses.

Union stewards can't be everywhere at once, and they can't personally see or hear everything that goes on the workplace. So part of your job as an individual union member is to be on the lookout for things that the union needs to know about, and to pass along the necessary information, especially since time is often of the essence. For example, if a change is made in working conditions but too many days pass before a grievance is filed, it may be too late to challenge the employer's unilateral action. So it's part of your responsibility as an individual union member to be the union's "eyes and ears" in your workplace.

Show Solidarity

It's pretty easy to understand in the abstract the notion that "an injury to one is an injury to all." And it's also not too complicated to grasp that if I don't speak up when someone else is being mistreated, that person isn't likely to be there for me when I need some support.

What's needed, of course, is for each of us to "walk the walk" and not just "talk the talk." When your co-workers on the night shift are getting cheated out of their differential, the test is whether you and your co-workers on the day shift make it your business to make sure that the union can do what's needed to take on the employer and support your coworkers on the night shift.

And solidarity extends outside of your workplace, too. If your or another union needs some bodies on a picket line or a large showing at a political or community event to support a fight at another workplace, you need to pitch in. Solidarity is about helping your fellow union members when they need it. Sometimes it may not seem like much, but stopping by a picket line to show your support means the world to men and women who are picketing or striking. And most of the time the favor will get returned in a very direct way when your picket line tomorrow is joined by the strikers you backed up yesterday. But even without such a one-to-one tradeoff, it's clear that building the overall union movement is part of what strengthens your union's rights in your workplace as well.

Be a Union Emissary

One of your union steward's responsibilities is to greet new employees and fill them in on the union. You can supplement this function very effectively by making a point of talking to newly hired workers about your personal experiences with the union and encouraging them to sign up. Having the union talked up by someone who is not a union official can go a long way toward creating the needed state of mind that the union is "us."

Your role as a union ambassador is perhaps even more critical outside the workplace. There are a lot of popular misconceptions about what unions are and what they do. You don't have to look far to find people buying into stereo-types that portray unions as consisting of nothing but fat cat bureaucrats living the good life off of hard-earned dues dollars and cutting self-serving deals with employers and politicians.

Though stereotypes may contain a grain of truth, this negative image is not at all an accurate depiction of the reality of labor unions today. Why is the public perception of the labor union movement so at odds with the day-to-day reality? A large part of the explanation is that the vast majority of Americans.are not represented by a labor union, and many Americans have never had any direct experience in a unionized workplace. In addition, anti-union employers and pol-iticians deliberately promote these negative stereotypes, to try and keep unions on the defensive. With little firsthand knowledge to go on, some people easily buy into the twisted version of things presented by employers and their allies in positions of wealth and power.

To increase public support for unions and the causes inside and out of the workplace that we fight for, it's important for people to have an accurate view of the role that unions play. And this is where you come in: if you make a point of letting friends and neighbors know about your own experiences as a unionized employee, this can be an effective way to correct popular distortions about the labor movement. This doesn't have to be done in a particularly formal way; tweet-ing and posting on social media are quick, easy ways to get the message across to lots of people. Or you can do something as simple as including "Unions: The Folks Who Brought You the Weekend" on your signature block.

Sometimes the most effective way to educate others as to the realities of unions is to enlist their support directly in a union fight at your or another work-place. Think about asking members of community or religious groups you are involved in, or your neighbors or others, to sign a petition, show up on a picket line, or make phone calls in support of a union effort in your community or else-where. The act of trying to persuade others to take such action may be the most direct way to get the dialogue going that will educate them as to the important role that unions play in society.

Get Involved

Part of the work that unions do is accomplished, at least in larger unions, by paid union staff members who earn their living conducting arbitration hearings, bargaining contracts, signing up members, and doing all of the other jobs that make a union effective. And some tasks are taken care of by stewards and union officers who may get some time off or some additional compensation to do their union work.

But the resources of any union are limited, and there is always much more that unions could do to be even more effective in defending the members' interests. A union's power is unleashed when individual members take it upon themselves to pitch in and each does a little something to contribute to the larger effort. No matter what kind of person you are, you have something you can contribute to make your union stronger. If you have good communication skills, you might volunteer to write for the local newsletter or website, or to beef up your union's presence on social media. If you have some expertise in health care benefits or health and safety matters, you might volunteer to serve on a committee or help out during contract negotiations. If you like photography, you can volunteer to photograph a union event. At the very least, we've all got at least a little time to spare once or twice a month, so why not volunteer to help hand-deliver union literature to your fellow employees, as a way of getting some conversations going?

Work for Change

In the larger society in which we live, sometimes things aren't working well at all and quite a bit of effort is needed to turn things around. Citizens sometimes have to organize among themselves, going door-to-door to enlist the support of others in the community to "throw out the bums" at election time, or to straighten out a nonresponsive school board or another group making decisions that affect us.

You may be in a similar situation in your workplace life. You may have had the feeling reading parts of this book that the descriptions of how unions work on behalf of their members to improve working conditions sound good but don't fully match up to the reality that you have experienced. But just as in the larger society, the solution is not simply to give up. Unions, like societies, ultimately are democratic, and change for the better is always possible.

So if your situation is that all is not well within your union, what are the steps that you need to take? First, educate yourself as to how the union is supposed to work. The information discussed earlier on union constitutions and bylaws, and the various laws that govern union activities, should give you a good starting point for understanding what your union ought to be doing, and your rights to have a say.

Second, the key to success always lies in collective action. If you are dissatisfied with how your union goes about its business, then others must be, as well. Find co-workers who want to bring about change and figure out together what can be done. Sometimes, the solution is no more difficult than communicating with the proper individuals in positions of responsibility in the union. Make sure they understand why you're dissatisfied and the efforts you're willing to pitch in on to improve things. Other times, of course, you will encounter a great deal more resistance. Ultimately, it may be necessary to "organize" within the union, and to become an alternative voice. You and like-minded co-workers may need to attend and speak up at union meetings and actively campaign to turn things around. You may end up deciding to run for union office yourself, and to engage in one-on-one organizing to "get out the vote."

No person is perfect, no organization is perfect, and no society is perfect. But all of us are capable of becoming better people than we were yesterday, and we all strive to do so. Similarly, no matter how messy things may sometimes appear to be in the larger society, we try to bring about improvements to make things better for all.

Our unions are no different. None are perfect, but all are capable of being improved. Take what you have learned from this book and use it as a starting point to become a voice and presence in your union.

The union is you and your co-workers; you have it within your power to make your union an ever-more-effective fighter for workplace rights and justice.

ACKNOWLEDGEMENTS

If this book renders a service to the union movement, thanks are due to my two publishers. David Prosten of Union Communication Services saw a need and decided to fill it, and the first edition of this book was the result. His encouragement as an editor and scrupulously fair dealings as a publisher showed me what a valuable part of the labor movement he is, and what a fine human being, too. Tim Sheard and Hard Ball Press stepped in to shepherd the second edition, aided and abetted by the able copy editor Joe Fedele.

The task of writing and later revising this book was work, no doubt about it, but it was personally fulfilling. My career path gave me a breadth of knowledge about America labor unions, since I'd chosen to perform such a wide range of union work. I began as a lawyer with the National Labor Relations Board, then moved on to lawyering, bargaining, and organizing with unions representing many different types of public and private sector workers: the American Federation of State, County and Municipal Employees, the National Education Association, the National Treasury Employees Union, the Newspaper Guild, and the Service Employees International Union – before settling in for a couple of decades with the American Association of University Professors. As the years went by I increasingly devoted time to university-based labor education, teaching at the University of Illinois, the (sadly, now defunct) National Labor College, and most recently at Ton Duc Thang University in Ho Chi Minh City. I like to think my breadth of experience in the labor movement prepared me for the task of writing this book.

When David first approached me with the book idea and years later when Tim expressed interest in producing a second edition, I learned how fortunate I was to be dealing with principled fellow members of the National Writers Union, UAW Local 1981. There was no need for me to arm myself to negotiate fair book contracts. They both treated their union brother scrupulously fairly, for which I'm appreciative.

I've had the privilege of working with a lot of smart and dedicated union activists, and I'm grateful to all who taught me through the years. To three who were kind enough to review my initial manuscript and to help me improve it, I offer special thanks: my former AAUP colleagues Ernie Benjamin and Pat Shaw, and the late Jeff Lustig, professor at Cal State-Sacramento, and activist in his union, the California Faculty Association. To the readers, I assure you that whatever errors of commission, omission, fact or presentation that appear here are my responsibility alone.

Like most of us in the union movement, I've gotten the motivation and inspiration needed to fight the good fight from a number of different sources. For over four decades, my thinking and my actions have been shaped in great measure by two invaluable lessons: that limits are not ascertainable and truths not readily apparent. For holding the doors open for me over the years, I offer gratitude to my shotokan karate teachers, most particularly Masataka Mori Sensei.

Finally, the family environment I grew up in and the ones I was fortunate enough to create with my children and their families have given me what I needed to keep plugging away in the union movement. So my gratitude, in large doses, extends to my mom, Millie Mauer (who showed me early on, by example, that the perceived limits are not the real ones), and to Marc Mauer, who's never stopped being my inspirational big brother. And I can't summon the words to convey my love and admiration for Jan Fritz, my beloved life companion, and for Jossi and Matthew Fritz-Mauer, the two greatest guys that ever were.

GLOSSARY

The world of unions has its own vocabulary. Some words or phrases are used solely within this world, while others may have a slightly different meaning when you encounter them elsewhere. Here is a list of some of the more important parts of the union vocabulary. For a more comprehensive guide to labor terms see *The Lexicon of Labor* by R. Emmett Murray (New York: The New Press, 2010.)

AFL-CIO: the national federation that includes most American labor unions, resulting from the 1955 merger of the American Federation of Labor and the Congress of Industrial Organizations.

agency fee: a fee, usually somewhat lower than the full dues amount, that non-members are required to pay to the union. The payment covers the costs of the representation services that the union provides.

agency shop: see union shop.

arbitration: the process by which a neutral outside party acts as a "judge," taking evidence and issuing a binding ruling on a contract grievance or other dispute.

bargaining: the process of face-to-face meetings, exchange of proposals, and give and take that produces a union contract.

bargaining team: the union or employer group of individuals that goes to the bargaining table for formal negotiations.

bargaining unit: the group of employees represented by a particular union, and usually covered by a single union contract.

branch: *see* union local.

Central Labor Councils: the AFL-CIO-sponsored collection of the local unions in a particular city or other geographical area.

chapter: *see* union local

collective bargaining: *see* bargaining

collective bargaining agreement: the document produced as a result of negotiations between a union and an employer, constituting the set of binding workplace rules.

constitution and bylaws: the governing documents of a local union or higher up union body.

contract: *see* collective bargaining agreement

corporate campaign: a multifaceted pressure campaign waged by a union, designed to exploit an employer's legal weaknesses, public relations vulnerabilities, or business bottom line.

dues: the money paid by union members to finance the costs of running the union.

duty of fair representation (DFR): the union's obligation to act diligently and fairly in the interests of members of the bargaining unit. This flows from the union's role as the exclusive representative of all those in the bargaining unit.

enabling legislation: a law that grants the right to unionize to public sector employees

Equal Employment Opportunity Commission (EEOC): the federal agency that implements many discrimination laws. Many states and localities have equivalent agencies.

Employee Retirement Income Security Act (ERISA): the law governing most private employers' pension and welfare benefit plans

Fair Labor Standards Act (FLSA): the federal law setting the minimum wage and establishing standards for overtime pay. Many states and localities also have laws applicable in their jurisdictions.

Family and Medical Leave Act (FMLA): the 1993 law creating an entitlement to unpaid leave connected with family emergencies and medical situations.

Federal Labor Relations Authority: the equivalent of the National Labor Relations Board for federal sector employees, administering the federal labor law as it applies to those employed by the federal government.

Global Union Federations (GUF): the international organizations that coordinate the efforts of the various unions worldwide that represent employees in particular industries or types of work.

good cause: see just cause

grandfathering: when there is a change in a workplace rule or job benefit, but employees already on board are permitted to remain under the old rule.

grievance procedure: a series of steps set forth in a union contract for attempting to resolve disputes between the employer and employees/the union.

impasse: a deadlock in contract negotiations.

interest-based bargaining (IBB): an alternative form of negotiations, premised on jointly identifying problems and then finding solutions that benefit both sides.

International: usually refers to the national level of an American union, as in International Brotherhood of Teamsters, so named because of members in Puerto Rico, Canada, or elsewhere.

just cause: the usual standard for discipline, requiring sufficient and fair grounds before punishing an employee.

Labor Management Reporting and Disclosure Act (LMRDA): a federal law containing the Bill of Rights of Members of Labor Organizations, guaranteeing union members' right to participate in union meetings, to vote in union elections, and so on.

lodge: *see* union local

lockout: a refusal by an employer to allow employees to report to work, designed to force the union to accept the employer's position in a bargaining dispute.

mediation: the process by which a neutral person attempts to help the union and an employer resolve a bargaining or other dispute.

mutual-gains bargaining: *see* interest-based bargaining

National Labor Relations Board (NLRB): the federal agency that administers the National Labor Relations Act, the labor law that applies to most private sector employees.

negotiated agreement: *see* collective bargaining agreement

negotiating team: *see* bargaining team

negotiations: *see* bargaining

Occupational Safety and Health Administration (OSHA): the federal agency that administers the basic health and safety law.

open shop: a workplace where union membership and payment of dues or other fees to the union are voluntary.

organizing: "external organizing" refers to acquiring union rights for unrepresented employees; "internal organizing" means persuading nonmembers to join the union that already represents them.

past practice: a procedure or workplace custom that can acquire binding effect.

private sector: privately owned companies and their employees.

public sector: government employment at all levels, including state, county, city and other localities.

Railway Labor Act: the labor law covering the transportation industry, with rules on organizing and bargaining that differ substantially from those of the National Labor Relations Act.

ratification: the procedure in which union members vote to accept or reject a negotiated contract settlement.

receiverships: see trusteeships

redcircling: see grandfathering

retaliation: punitive action taken against an employee for exercising a contractual or legal right.

"right to work": legislation prohibiting various types of union security arrangements. In jurisdictions covered by such laws, unions cannot require nonmembers to make a financial payment to cover any of the union's costs of operation.

steward: the front-line union representative, usually a volunteer, who is responsible for giving guidance on workplace rights, filing grievances, and other representation and organizing tasks.

seniority: A worker's length of service with an employer relative to the length of service of other workers. Contracts frequently use seniority to determine layoffs, promotions, recalls and transfers.

state federation: the body bringing together various unions in a state, so they can combine forces for effective action at the state level.

strike: a collective refusal to work, designed to pressure an employer to accept the union's position in a bargaining or other dispute.

trusteeships: placing the day-to-day running of a union local in the hands of a higher union body, usually as a result of financial irregularities or extreme mismanagement.

unfair labor practice (ULP): a labor law violation, committed by either an employer or a union. Common employer violations include making changes in the workplace without going through the union, and interfering with employees' rights to engage in union activity.

union contract: *see* collective bargaining agreement

union local: the lowest level in a union's formal organizational structure, usually consisting of employees in a particular workplace or city.

union security / (or "union shop" or "agency shop"): workplace arrangements where new employees are required either to join the union or to pay a "fair share" fee to the union to compensate it for direct representation and other services.

Wagner Act: the 1935 federal statute, subsequently amended (as the National Labor Relations Act), that set up the framework for union representation for most private sector employees; named for U.S. Senator Robert F. Wagner of New York (1877-1953).

162

Weingarten rights: an employee's right to have a representative present when being questioned about a possible disciplinary infraction. Named for a 1975 United States Supreme Court decision, *NLRB* v. *J. Weingarten, Inc.*

whistleblower: an employee who gives information to the public, the news media, or government agency about some employer activity that the employee believes is illegal or improper.

win-win bargaining: *see* interest-based bargaining

workers' compensation: the government-regulated insurance scheme providing for set monetary payments to employees who are injured or disabled in connection with their jobs.

HELPFUL CONTACTS

I hope this book has made you interested in learning more about unions and workplace rights, or in becoming more active in the union movement. Your own union is the best place to start, but there are many other groups to learn from and get materials from. The following list offers a broad sampling of the possibilities.

AFL-CIO (the nation's primary labor federation; links to affiliated unions)
815 16th St., NW
Washington, DC 20006
Phone: (202) 637-5000
www.aflcio.org

American Civil Liberties Union (information on workplace rights)
125 Broad St., 18th Floor
New York, NY 10004
Phone: (212) 549-2500
www.aclu.org

A. Phillip Randolph Institute (African-American unionists)
1444 Eye St., NW, 3rd Floor
Washington, DC 20005
Phone: (202) 289-2774
www.aprihq.org

Asian Pacific American Labor Alliance (Asian Pacific unionists)

815 16th St., NW

Washington, DC 20006

Phone: (202) 842-1263

www.apalanet.org

Association for Union Democracy (internal union democracy)

500 State St.

Brooklyn, NY 11217

Phone: (718) 855-6650

Fax: (718) 855- 6799

www.uniondemocracy.org

Coalition of Black Trade Unionists (African-American unionists)

PO Box 66268

Washington, DC 20035

Phone: (202) 429-1203

Fax: (202) 429-1102

www.cbtu.org

Coalition of Labor Union Women (women unionists)

1126 16th St., NW

Washington, DC 20036

Phone: (202) 466-4610

Fax: (202) 776-0537

www.cluw.org

Department of Labor (wages and hours, family and medical leave, plant closings)

200 Constitution Ave., NW

Washington, DC 20210

Phone: (202) 219-6666

www.dol.gov

Equal Employment Opportunity Commission (discrimination)
1801 L St., NW
Washington, DC 20507
Phone: (202) 663-4900
www.eeoc.gov

Federal Labor Relations Authority (unfair labor practices, union representation elections for federal sector employees)
607 14th St., NW, Suite 210
Washington, DC 20424
Phone: (202) 482-6690
www.flra.gov

Government Accountability Project (whistleblower protection group)
1612 K St., NW
Washington, DC 20006
Phone: (202) 408-0034
www.whistleblower.org

Jobs With Justice (coalition efforts for workers' rights campaigns)
501 3rd St., NW
Washington, DC 20001
Phone: (202) 434-1106
www.igc.org/jwj

Labor Council for Latin American Advancement (Latin American unionists)
815 16th St., NW
Washington, DC 20006
Phone: (202) 347-4223
www.lclaa.org

Labor Heritage Foundation (music and arts for the union cause)
1925 K St., NW Suite 400
Washington, DC 20006
Phone: (202)842-7880
www.laborheritage.org

Labornet (independent information source for labor news and views)
www.labornet.org

Labor Notes (news of rank-and-file activism)
7435 Michigan Ave.
Detroit, MI 48210
Phone: (313) 842-6262
www.labornotes.org

Labor Research Association (news and analysis covering the labor movement and the economy)
145 West 28th St.
New York, NY 10001
Phone: (212) 714-1677
www.laborresearch.org

Legal Information Institute (links to employment and labor laws of all fifty states, the District of Columbia and Puerto Rico)
www.law.cornell.edu/topics/Table_Labor.htm

National Employment Lawyers Association (links to labor law sites)
www.nela.org

National Labor Relations Board (unfair labor practices, union representation elections for private sector employees)
1015 Half Street SE,
Washington, DC 20570-0001
Phone: (202) 273-1000
www.nlrb.gov

Occupational Safety and Health Administration (health and safety)
U.S. Department of Labor
200 Constitution Ave., NW
Washington, DC 20210

Phone: (800) 356-4674
www.osha.gov

Pride At Work (mutual support between the labor movement and the gay, lesbian and transgender community)
815 16th St., NW
Room 4020
Washington, DC 20006
Phone: (202) 637-5085
www.prideatwork.org

Union Jobs Clearinghouse (job openings in the labor movement)
www.unionjobs.com

Union Label Department, AFL-CIO (information on union-made products and services)
815 16th St., NW
Washington, DC 20006
Phone: (202) 628-2131
www.unionlabel.org

Union Privilege (labor-sponsored credit cards, auto club, etc.)
1125 15th St., NW
Suite 300
Washington, DC 20005
Phone: (202) 293-5330
www.unionpriv.org

DIRECTORY OF UNIONS

The following list gives contact information on all major unions in the United States, including every one affiliated with the AFL-CIO, and many—but not all—of the country's independent unions, as well as some other related organizations and professional associations.

1199SEIU
310 West 43rd Street
New York, NY 10036
Phone: (212) 582-1890
Web: www.1199seiu.org

Actors & Artistes of America, Associated
165 West 46th St.
New York, NY 10036
Phone: (212) 869-8530
Web: www.actorsequity.org

Airline Pilots Association (ALPA)
1625 Massachusetts Ave., N.W.
Washington, DC 20036
Phone: (202) 797-4010
Web: www.alpa.org

American Association of University Professors (AAUP)
1012 14th St., N.W., Suite 500
Washington, DC 20005
Phone: (202) 737-5900
Web: www.aaup.org

American Guild of Musical Artists (AGMA)
1727 Broadway
New York, NY 10019
Phone: (212) 265-3687
Web: www.musicalartists.org/

American Guild of Variety Artists (AGVA)
184 Fifth Ave.
New York, NY 10010
Phone: (212) 675-1003
Web: www.agvausa.com/

American Nurses' Association (ANA)
600 Maryland Ave., S.W., Suite 100 West
Washington, DC 20024-2571
Phone: (202) 651-7000
Web: www.nursingworld.org

Automobile, Aerospace & Agricultural Implement Workers of America (UAW)
8000 E. Jefferson Ave.
Detroit, MI 48214
Phone: (313) 926-5000
Web: www.uaw.org

Bakery, Confectionary, Tobacco Workers and Grain Millers International Union (BCTGM)
10401 Connecticut Ave.
Kensington, MD 20895
Phone: (301) 933-8600
Web: www.bctgm.org

Boilermakers, Iron Ship Builders, Blacksmiths, Forgers and Helpers (IBB)
753 State Ave., Suite 570
Kansas City, KS 66101
Phone: (913) 371-2640
Web: www.boilermakers.org

Bricklayers and Allied Craftworkers, International Union of (BAC)
815 15th St., N.W.
Washington, DC 20005
Phone: (202) 783-3788
Web: www.bacweb.org

California School Employees Association (CSEA)
2045 Lundy Ave., PO Box 640
San Jose, CA 95106
Phone: (408) 263-8000
Web: www.csea.com

Carpenters & Joiners of America, United Brotherhood of (UBC)
101 Constitution Ave., N.W.
Washington, DC 20001
Phone: (202) 546-6206
Web: www.carpenters.org/

Christian Labor Association (CLA)
405 Centerstone Ct., PO Box 65
Zeeland, MI 49464
Phone: (616) 772-9164
Web: www.cla-usa.com

Communications Workers of America (CWA)
501 3rd St., N.W.
Washington, DC 20001
Phone: (202) 434-1100
Web: www.cwa-union.org

Electrical Workers, International Brotherhood of (IBEW)
1125 15th St., N.W.
Washington, DC 20005
Phone: (202) 833-7000
Web: www.ibew.org

Elevator Constructors, International Union of (IUEC)
5565 Sterrett Pl.
Columbia, MD 21044
Phone: (410) 997-9000
Web: www.iuec.org

Farm Workers of America, AFL-CIO, United (UFW)
29700 Woodford-Tehachapi Rd.
Keene, CA 93531
Phone: (661) 822-5571
Web: www.ufw.org

Fire Fighters, International Association of (IAFF)
1750 New York Ave., N.W.
Washington, DC 20006
Phone: (202) 737-8484
Web: www.iaff.org

Flight Attendants, Association of (AFA)
501 3rd Street NW, Washington, DC 20001
Phone: (202) 434-1300
Web: www. afacwa.org

Food and Commercial Workers International Union, United (UFCW)
1775 K St., N.W.
Washington, DC 20006

Phone: (202) 223-3111
Web: www.ufcw.org

International Union (GMP)
608 East Baltimore Pike
Media, PA 19063
Phone: (610) 565-5051
Web: www.gmpiu.org/

Government Employees, American Federation of
(AFGE)
80 F St., N.W.
Washington, DC 20001
Phone: (202) 737-8700
Web: www.afge.org

Graphic Artists Guild
90 John St., Ste. 403
New York, NY 10038-3202
Phone: (212) 791-3400
Web: www.gag.org

Graphic Communications International Union
(GCIU)
1900 L St., N.W.
Washington, DC 20036-4804
Phone: (202) 462-1400
Web: www.gciu.org

Horseshoers of US and Canada, International
Union of Journeymen
6920 Hitchcock Rd.
White Lake, MI 48383
Phone: (810) 887-5922
Web: www.americanfarriers.com

Independent Pilots Association (IPA)
200 Highrise Dr., Ste. 199
Louisville, KY 40213
Phone: (502) 968-0341
Web: www.ipapilot.org

Iron Workers, International Association of Bridge,
Structural & Ornamental
1750 New York Ave., N.W., Ste. 400
Washington, DC 20006
Phone: (202) 383-4800
Web: www.diro.com

Laborers' International Union of North America
(LIUNA)
905 16th St., N.W.
Washington, DC 20006
Phone: (202) 737-8320
Web: www.liuna.org

Letter Carriers, National Association of (NALC)
100 Indiana Ave., N.W.
Washington, DC 20001
Phone: (202) 393-4695
Web: www.nalc.org

Locomotive Engineers, Brotherhood of (BLE)
Standard Building, Mezzanine Level
1370 Ontario Ave.
Cleveland, OH 44113
Phone: (216) 241-2630
Web: www.ble.org

Longshoremen's and Warehousemen's Union,
International (ILWU)
1188 Franklin St.
San Francisco, CA 94109-6800
Phone: (415) 775-0533
Web: www.ilwu.org

Longshoremen's Association AFL-CIO,
International (ILA)
17 Battery Pl., Rm. 1530
New York, NY 10004
Phone: (212) 425-1200
Web: www.ila2000.org

Machinists and Aerospace Workers, International Association of (IAM)
9000 Machinists Pl.
Upper Marlboro, MD 20772
Phone: (301) 967-4500
Web: www.goiam.org

Maintenance of Way Employees, Brotherhood of (BWE)
26555 Evergreen Rd, Ste. 200
Southfield, MI 48076
Phone: (248) 948-1010
Web: www.bmwe.org

Marine Engineers' Beneficial Association (MEBA)
444 North Capitol St., N.W., Ste. 800
Washington, DC 20001
Phone: (202) 638-5355
Web: www.mebahq@d1meba.org

Maryland Classified Employees Association, Inc. (MCEA)
7127 Rutherford Rd.
Baltimore, MD 21207
Phone: (410) 298-8800
Web: www.mcea.org

Mine Workers of America, United (UMWA)
8315 Lee Hwy.
Fairfax, VA 22031
Phone: (703) 208-7200
Web: www.umwa.org

Montana Public Employees Association, Inc. (MONT-PEA)
PO Box 5600
Helena, MT 59604
Phone: (406) 442-4600
Web: www.mfpe.org/

Musicians of the US and Canada, American Federation of (AFM)
1501 Broadway, Ste. 600
New York, NY 10036
Phone: (212) 869-1330
Web: www.afm.org

National Air Traffic Controllers Association (NATCA)
1325 Massachusetts Ave., N.W.
Washington, DC 20005
Phone: (202) 628-5451
Web: www.natca.org

National Alliance of Postal and Federal Employees (NAPFE)
1628 11th St., N.W.
Washington, DC 20001
Phone: (202) 939-6325
Web: www.napfe.org

National Education Association (NEA)
1201 16th St., N.W.
Washington, DC 20036
Phone: (202) 833-4000
Web: www.nea.org

National Federation of Federal Employees (NFFE)
1225 New York Ave., NW, Suite 450
Washington, DC 20005
Phone: 202-216-4420
Web: www.nffe.org

National Fraternal Order of Police (FOP)
701 Marriott Drive
Nashville TN 37214
Web: www.fop.net

National Rural Letter Carriers' Association (NRLCA)
1630 Duke St., 4th Floor
Alexandria, VA 22314-3465

Phone: (703) 684-5545
Web: www.nrlca.org

National Treasury Employees Union (NTEU)
901 E St. N.W., Ste. 600
Washington, DC 20004
Phone: (202) 783-4444
Web: www.nteu.org

National Writers Union (NWU)
113 University Place, 6th Floor
New York, NY 10003
Phone: (212) 254-0279
Web: www.nwu.org

NewsGuild-CWA
501 Third St., NW, 6th floor
Washington, DC 20001-2797
Phone: 202-434-7177
Web: www.newsguild.org

Novelty and Production Workers, International
Union of Allied
1950 West Erie St.
Chicago, IL 60622
Phone: (312) 738-0822
Web: www.iuanpw.org/

Office and Professional Employees International
Union (OPEIU)
265 West 14th St., Ste. 610
New York, NY 10011
Phone: (212) 675-3210
Web: www.opeiu.org

Operating Engineers, International Union of
(IUOE)
1125 17th St., N.W.
Washington, DC 20036
Phone: (202) 429-9100
Web: www.iuoe.org

Operative Plasterers' & Cement Masons'
International Association
9700 Patuxent Woods Drive, Suite 200
Columbia, MD 21046
Phone (301) 623-1000
Web: www.opcmia.org

Oregon School Employees Association (OSEA)
4735 Liberty Rd. South, P.O. Box 4027
Salem, OR 97302
Phone: (503) 588-0121
Web: www.osea.org

Painters & Allied Trades of the US & Canada,
International Brotherhood of (IBPAT)
1750 New York Ave., N.W.
Washington, DC 20006
Phone: (202) 637-0700
Web: www.iupat.org

Police Associations, International Union of (IUPA)
1549 Ringling Blvd, 6th Floor
Sarasota, FL 34236
Phone: (800) 247-4872
Web: www.iupa.org

Postal Workers Union, AFL-CIO, American
(APWU)
1300 L St., N.W.
Washington, DC 20005
Phone: (202) 842-4200
Web: www.apwu.org

Professional and Technical Engineers, International
Federation of (IFPTE)
501 3rd Street, NW Suite 701
Washington DC 20001
phone (202) 239-4880
Web: www.ifpte.org

Professional Athletes, Federation of
2021 L St., N.W., 6th Fl.
Washington. DC 20036
Phone: (202) 463-2200
Web: www.dpeaflcio.org

Radio Association, American (ARA)
1600 Rabke Road
Canton, GA 30014
Phone (770) 592-3232
Web: www.americanradioassociation.org

Retail, Wholesale and Department Store Union
(RWDSU)
370 7th Ave, Ste 501
New York, New York 10001
(212) 684-5300
Web: www.rwdsu.info

Roofers, Waterproofers and Allied Workers, United
Union of
1660 L St., N.W., Ste. 800
Washington, DC 20036
Phone: (202) 463-7663
Web: www.unionroofers.com

School Administrators, American Federation of
(AFSA)
1729 21st St., N.W.
Washington, DC 20009
Phone: (202) 986-4209
Web: www.admin.org

SAG-AFTRA
5757 Wilshire Blvd.
Los Angeles, CA 90036
Phone: (213) 954-1600
Web: www.sagaftra.org

Seafarers International Union of North America
(SIU)
5201 Auth Way and Britannia Way
Camp Springs, MD 20746
Phone: (301) 899-0675
Web: www.seafarers.org

Service Employees International Union (SEIU)
1800 Massachusetts Ave., NW
Washington, DC 20036
Phone:(202) 898-3200
Web: www.seiu.org

Sheet Metal Workers International Association
(SMWIA)
1750 New York Ave., N.W.
Washington, DC 20006
Phone: (202) 783-5880
Web: www.smwia.org

Signalmen, Brotherhood of Railroad (BRS)
601 West Golf Rd., PO Box "U"
Mount Prospect, IL 60056
Phone: (847) 439-3732
Web: www.brs.org

South Dakota State Employees Organization
(SD-SEO)
PO Box 1021
Pierre, SD 57501
Phone: (605) 224-8241
Web: www.sdseo.org

Stage Employees & Moving Picture Techs, Artists &
Allied Crafts (IATSE)
1515 Broadway, Ste. 601
New York, NY 10036
Phone: (212) 730-1770
Web: www.iatse.net

State Employees Association of North Carolina, Inc. (SEANC)
PO Drawer 27727
Raleigh, NC 27611
Phone: (919) 833-6436
Web: www.seanc.org/

State, County and Municipal Employees, American Federation of (AFSCME)
1625 L St., N.W.
Washington, DC 20036
Phone: (202) 429-1000
Web: www.afscme.org

Steelworkers of America, United (USWA)
Five Gateway Center
Pittsburgh, PA 15222
Phone: (412) 562-2300
Web: www.uswa.org

Teachers, American Federation of (AFT)
555 New Jersey Ave., N.W.
Washington, DC 20001
Phone: (202) 879-4400
Web: www.aft.org

Teamsters, International Brotherhood of (IBT)
25 Louisiana Ave., N.W.
Washington, DC 20001
Phone: (202) 624-6800
Web: www.teamster.org

Train Dispatchers Association, American (ATDA)
1370 Ontario St., Ste. 1040
Cleveland, OH 44113
Phone: (216) 241-2770
Web: www.atda.org

Transit Union, Amalgamated (ATU)
5025 Wisconsin Ave., N.W., 3rd Floor
Washington, DC 20016

Phone: (202) 537-1645
Web: www.atu.org

Transport Workers Union of America (TWU)
80 West End Ave., 5th Floor
New York, NY 10023
Phone: (212) 873-6000
Web: www.twu.org

Transportation Communications Union / IAM (TCU)
3 Research Pl. Rockville, MD 20850
Phone: (301) 948-4910
Web: www.goiam.org/territories/tcu-union

Transportation Union, United (UTU)
14600 Detroit Ave.
Cleveland, OH 44107
Phone: (216) 228-9400
Web: www.utu.org

Union of Needletrades, Industrial and Textile Employees (UNITE HERE!)
275 7th Avenue
New York, NY 10001-6708
Phone: (212) 265-7000
Web: www.unitehere.org

United Association of Plumbing and Pipefitting Industry (UA)
901 Massachusetts Ave., N.W.
Washington, DC 20001
Phone: (202) 628-5823
Web: www.ua.org

United Auto Workers (UAW)
8000 East Jefferson Avenue
Detroit, Michigan 48214
Phone: (313) 926-5000
Web: www.uaw.org

United Electrical, Radio and Machine Workers of
America (UE)
One Gateway Ctr., Ste. 1400
Pittsburgh, PA 15222-1416
Phone: (412) 471-8919
Web: www.ueunion.org

Utah Public Employees' Association (UPEA)
1000 W Bellwood Ln.
Murray, UT 84123
Phone: (801) 264-8732
Web: www.upea.net

Utah School Employees Association (USEA)
864 East Arrowhead Ln.
Murray, UT 84107-5211
Phone: (801) 269-9320
Web: www.useautah.org

Utility Workers Union of America (UWUA)
300 L. Street, N.W., Suite 1200
Washington, DC 20005
Phone: (202) 899-2851
Web: www.uwua.net

LABOR THEMED FILMS

Here's just a small selection of movies that show how working life looks from the ground level up, and the role that unions have played in transforming the American workplace.

10,000 Black Men Named George
"The True Story of a Railroad Revolution": A Philip Randolph's fight to organize the Pullman porters (all of whom were Black men, and all of whom were referred to as "George").

American Dream
Documentary on the hard-fought, but unsuccessful meatpackers' strike against Hormel in the 1980's.

At The River I Stand
The story of the Memphis sanitation workers' strike, and Dr. Martin Luther King's last days in support of that struggle.

Blue Collar
Thriller starring Richard Pryor, Harvey Keitel and Yaphet Kotto as Detroit autoworkers who uncover some dangerous information about their union.

Bread and Roses
Dramatic telling of the unionization story of janitorial workers in Los Angeles; inspired by the Service Employees International Union's pathbreaking Justice for Janitors campaign.

F.I.S.T.
Fictionalized account of Jimmy Hoffa's rise in the Teamsters, starring Sylvester Stallone.

Harlan County USA
Oscar-winning documentary on a United Mine Workers' battle in Kentucky in the 1970's.

Hoffa
Jack Nicholson stars as Jimmy Hoffa, in this fictionalized biography.

Live Nude Girls Unite!
Entertaining documentary on the first successful effort to unionize by "exotic dancers."

Made in Dagenham
Dramatization of an English strike that brought to the fore the issue of equal pay for women.

Modern Times
The Charlie Chaplin comedy classic, in which "The Little Tramp" struggles against the oppression of industrialization of the workplace.

Matewan
Dramatization of racial and class conflict in a bloody coal miners' struggle in the early days of unionization in West Virginia.

Norma Rae
Sally Field's Academy Award-winning performance as Crystal Lee Sutton, who led the fight to organize J.P. Stevens' textile workers in North Carolina.

North Country
Charlize Theron in the true-life story of the iron miner who won a landmark case on sexual harassment.

On The Waterfront
This is indisputedly the best film ever made about worker organizing. (Well, in the opinion of the author, at least.) Winner of eight Academy Awards, including best actor for Marlon Brando, this is the story of the fight against mob violence on the Hoboken, New Jersey docks.

Pride

This comedy / drama is based on the true story of the unlikely – but successful – mutual support between London gay and lesbian activists and striking Welsh miners.

Silkwood

Meryl Streep as Karen Silkwood, the union activist who blew the whistle on dangerous conditions in the nuclear industry, and then died under suspicious circumstances in a car crash.

Salt of the Earth

The true story of a Mexican-American miners' strike in New Mexico, with a theme of equity: for the immigrant miners to earn the same wages as Anglos, and for the miners' wives to participate as equals on the picket line. Most of the roles in the film are played by the actual miners and their wives.

The Molly Maguires

Sean Connery took a break from playing James Bond to star in this fictionalized account of a secret group of Irish immigrant coal miners at the end of the 19th century who used sabotage and murder to fight back against cruel conditions in the Pennsylvania coal mines.

INDEX

ABOUT THE AUTHOR

Michael Mauer began his labor relations career in the 1970's as an attorney with the National Labor Relations Board. He has since held a variety of legal, bargaining and organizing positions with unions representing both public and private sector workers, including serving as director of organizing and services for the American Association of University Professors and collective bargaining director for the Service Employees International Union (SEIU). He has taught and conducted training for the AFL-CIO's National Labor College and in the labor studies programs at the University of Illinois at Urbana-Champaign and at Ton Duc Thang University in Ho Chi Minh City, Vietnam. His other publications include *Academic Collective Bargaining* (Ernst Benjamin, coeditor), New York, MLA, (2006).

Titles fom Hard Ball Press

A Great Vision – A Militant Family's Journey Through the Twentieth Century – by Richard March
Caring – 1199 Nursing Home Workers Tell Their Story
Fight For Your Long Day – Classroom Edition, by Alex Kudera
Good Trouble: A Shoeleather History of Nonviolent
Direct Action, Steve Thornton
I Still Can't Fly: Confessions of a Lifelong Troublemaker,
Kevin John Carroll
Legacy Costs: The Story of a Factory Town, Richard Hudelson
Love Dies, a thriller, by Timothy Sheard
The Man Who Fell From the Sky, Bill Fletcher, Jr.
Murder of a Post Office Manager, A Legal Thriller, by Paul Felton
New York Hustle – Pool Rooms, School Rooms and Street Corners, a memoir, Stan Maron
Passion's Pride – Return to the Dawning, Cathie Wright- Lewis
The Secrets of the Snow, a book of poetry, Hiva Panahi
Sixteen Tons, a Novel, by Kevin Corley
The Union Member's Complete Guide, Michael Mauer
Throw Out the Water, a novel, by Kevin Corley
What Did You Learn at Work Today?, by Helena Worthen
Welcome to the Union, by Michael Mauer
With Our Loving Hands, 1199 Nursing Home Workers Tell Their Story, Steve Bender, Ed.
Wining Richmond, Gayle McLaughlin
With Our Loving Hands – 1199 Nursing Home Workers Tell Their Story
Woman Missing, A Mill Town Mystery, by Linda Nordquist

THE LENNY MOSS MYSTERIES by Timothy Sheard

This Won't Hurt A Bit
Some Cuts Never Heal
A Race Against Death
No Place To Be Sick
Slim To None
A Bitter Pill
Someone Has To Die

CHILDREN'S BOOKS

The Cabbage That Came Back, Stephen Pearl (author), Rafael Pearl (Illustrator), Sara Pearl (translator)

Good Guy Jake, Mark Torres (author), Yana Podrieez (Illustrator), Madelin Arroyo (translator)

Hats Off For Gabbie, Marivir Montebon (author), Yana Podriez (illustrator), Madelin Arroyo (translator)

Jimmy's Carwash Adventure, Victor Narro (author & translator), Yana Podriez (illustrator)

Joelito's Big Decision, Ann Berlak (author), Daniel Camacho (Illustrator), José Antonio Galloso (Translator)

Manny & The Mango Tree, Ali R. Bustamante (author), Monica Lunot-Kuker (illustrator), Mauricio Niebla (translator)

Margarito's Forest, Andy Carter (author), Allison Havens (illustrator), Omar Mejia (Translator)

Trailer Park – Jennifer Dillard (author), Madelin Arroyo (translator), Anna Usacheva *(Illustrations)*

Made in the USA
Coppell, TX
02 September 2023

21119891R00120